PALERMO'S STREET MARKETS ⭐ 7

A feast for the eyes and ears:
Palermo's markets offer
Mediterranean delicacies all
day long.
📷 *Tip: Chat with the traders, buy
a little something and many will
be more than happy to pose for a
photo.*

➤ p. 84, The North Coast

DUOMO DI MONREALE ⭐ 8

Covering an area of 6,340m², the
cathedral's gold-coloured mosaics
tell stories from the Bible; in the
cloister, 208 capitals proclaim the
theology of the Middle Ages.

➤ p. 85, The North Coast

VALLE DEI TEMPLI ⭐ 9

The 2,500-year-old city of Akragas
(now Agrigento) draws in visitors
with the splendour of its Greek
temples.
📷 *Tip: Templi illuminati – at
dusk the camera lens plays with
the columned architecture.*

➤ p. 104, The Southwest

STROMBOLI ⭐ 10

Experience the nocturnal volcanic
fireworks close to the summit
(photo).
📷 *Tip: Take a photo of the
glowing red Sciara del Fuoco
on a night-time boat trip.*

➤ p. 116, The Aeolian Islands

CONTENTS

THE AEOLIAN ISLANDS

THE NORTH COAST

THE NORTHEAST

THE SOUTHWEST

THE SOUTHEAST

CONTENTS

☼   Plan your visit   🛍 Shopping

€-€€€ Price categories   🍸 Going out

🍴   Eating & drinking   🏖 Top beaches

(🕮 A2) Refers to the removable pull-out map
(0) Located off the map

BEST OF
SICILY

Sun-kissed citrus trees backed by a view of snow-dusted Mount Etna

BEST ☂

WHEN IT RAINS

ACTIVITIES TO BRIGHTEN YOUR DAY

PLATES & BOWLS
When it rains, the bright tiles on the walls of the *Museo della Ceramica* in Caltagirone are especially lovely. Inside, the hundreds of tiles, vases, bowls, plates, jugs and figures dating from antiquity to the present day are a sight to behold.
➤ p. 65, The Southeast

ARCHAEOLOGY UNDER COVER
The colourful floor mosaics (photo) in the former *Villa Romana del Casale* near Piazza Armerina cover 4,100m² and have been roofed over.
➤ p. 66, The Southeast

**TO THE OPERA HOUSE
FOR COFFEE**
Sip a cappuccino in the *Caffè del Teatro* at Palermo's *Teatro Massimo,* Italy's largest opera house; then marvel at the magnificent decorations during a tour afterwards.
➤ p. 80, The North Coast

COOK LIKE MAMMA
Take lessons in Sicilian cooking from a passionate *signora* who will teach you the best way to prepare classics such as *maccheroni*, *involtini* and *pasta alla norma*, for example at *Agriturismo Gelso* in the Madonie mountains.
➤ p. 88, The North Coast

OFF TO THE SPA
Soak in the 38°C warm spa water in *Terme Segestane* and you won't even notice that it's raining! Pure bliss in the evening after a long day out.
➤ p. 97, The Southwest

SPIRIT OF WINE
Taste your way through orange liquors from Etna, the Nero d'Avola wines along the Cerasuolo di Vittoria wine route or the traditional Marsala wine from *Cantino Marco de Bartoli*. Meet new people and enjoy the surroundings with *winerytastingsicily.com*.
➤ p. 99, The Southwest

BEST ON A BUDGET

FOR SMALLER WALLETS

THROUGH THE EYES OF A PAINTER

Inside the church of *Santa Lucia al Sepolcro*, Lucia, the patron saint of Syracuse, lies martyred on the ground while two burly men dig her grave. Painted in 1608 in haunting chiaroscuro by Caravaggio, who had fled to Sicily after committing murder.
➤ p. 62, The Southeast

TEA-TIME

You can find out everything to do with tea in the feng shui-styled *La Casa del Tè* in Raddusa. Admission is free and, if you want to contribute, you can buy a small tea souvenir and support one of the *casa*'s charity projects.
➤ p. 66, The Southeast

PUBLIC TRANSPORT IN PALERMO

Palermo by bus is very affordable. Choose between a regular ticket, valid for 1½ hours (1.40 euros, or 1.80 euros if bought on the bus), or day tickets

(1–7 days; 1 day 3.50 euros, 3 days 8 euros, 7 days 16.50 euros). Buy tickets in advance at *tabacchi* shops. *amat.pa.it*
➤ p. 78, The North Coast

TAPPING THE SOURCE

Help yourself to mineral water directly from the spring at the crenellated *village fountain* outside the mountain village of Geraci Siculo. Take your own bottle and a bit of patience, as you'll have to wait your turn.
➤ p. 89, The North Coast

OPEN-AIR GALLERY IN A RIVER VALLEY

Take a brisk walk rather than standing in a museum queue: the modern *Fiumara d'Arte*, with its large sculptures that can be seen from some distance, including a pyramid and a labyrinth (photo), is in the hills above the Messina–Palermo coast road and in the rocky riverbeds of the dried-up River Tusa.
➤ p. 89, The North Coast

BEST
WITH CHILDREN

FUN FOR YOUNG & OLD

GELATI, GELATI

When it comes to training the palate, you can't start early enough: Sicily is ice cream paradise. Teach your child to say *"un gelato cioccolato per favore"*, and they are set for life.

KID'S MENU? DON'T BE SILLY!

While *bambini* may be frowned upon in an upscale *ristorante*, they are welcomed with open arms in any trattoria and are generally allowed to tuck into the same dishes as their parents (possibly with a few euros knocked off the bill).

SPLASH & SWIM

Sicily's longest strip of sand begins south of Syracuse and runs almost the entire length of the south coast. Or, for something a bit different, spend a fun afternoon at *Spray Park* near Taormina.

➤ p. 52, The Northeast

KEEPS YOU ON YOUR TOES

With much clanging of swords, the *puppet theatre* stages knightly legends featuring battles against the Saracens and the courtship of the beautiful Angelica. Watch in Syracuse and Palermo.

➤ p. 63, The Southeast & p. 84, The North Coast

ME & MY DONKEY

Child-friendly donkey rides (at *Agrimilo Donkey Breeding Sanctuary*) or pony tours on the slopes of Etna (with *Etna Donkey Trekking*) can make for a wonderful day out.

➤ p. 69, The Southeast & p. 46, The Northeast

FULL-SIZE PLAYTIME

At the port of Lipari, an entire church, the *Chiesa delle Anime del Purgatorio*, has been transformed into a "doll's house". Fun for all the family!

➤ p. 113, The Aeolian Islands

BEST ⚐

CLASSIC EXPERIENCES

ONLY IN SICILY

SWORDFISH SWORDS & BLOOD ORANGES

Mutton heads, squid, artichoke pyramids and the shouts of market traders: Catania's *fish market* and the *del Capo* and *Ballarò street markets* (photo) in Palermo stimulate the senses. If you can't stomach the idea of a calf's foot decorated with myrtle twigs, at least feast on the banquet with your eyes.
➤ p. 44, The Northeast, and p. 84, The North Coast

WILD PAPYRUS

Wild papyrus may be long extinct in Egypt, but it has been native to Sicily since Arab times. Pretend you're a pharaoh on your barge as you glide down the *River Ciane* on a boat trip.
➤ p. 64, The Southeast

A CAP WITH A HISTORY

Fashion designers have rediscovered the *coppola*, the hard-wearing Sicilian peaked cap that was once a symbol of the Mafia. Young Sicilian women opt for colourful velvet or all in white to go with a wedding dress. Whatever your taste, the cult shop is *Tanto di Coppola* in Palermo.
➤ p. 83, The North Coast

VEG TO GO

The real *caponata* – made of aubergines, celery, capers, green olives, wild fennel, tomatoes and honey – is eaten cold. Farmers take it with them to the fields. Try this classic *cucina povera* at the trattoria *San Giovanni* in Gela.
➤ p. 107, The Southwest

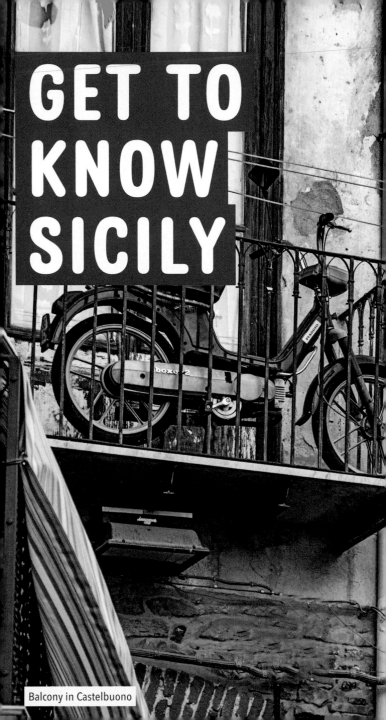

GET TO KNOW SICILY

Balcony in Castelbuono

DISCOVER SICILY

Over 2,400 years old: the Concordia temple in the Valle dei Templi near Agrigento

"Araaaance!" echoes singsong through the old town alley. Shutters are thrown open; widows dressed in black appear on balconies and lower their shopping baskets. The scent of oranges mingles with the smell of swordfish in garlic from a *trattoria* with bright fluorescent lights… This picture-book Sicily of old really does still exist, but be careful not to take it at total face value, or you might just miss its connection to the present.

PARTY STRIPS AND INSTAGRAM SHOTS

At Taormina, the one real tourist hotspot on the island with its view of Etna, five-star luxury hotels are appearing all over the place – as they did during the Belle Époque. Guests frequently include wealthy weekenders from larger cities. However, there are few tourists to be found during the lively and loud student-led *movida* celebrations that rampage through Catania's lava stone *centro storico* on summer evenings.

800–580 BCE
Founding of many Phoenician and Greek towns

241 BCE–CE 468
Becomes a Roman province

CE 535–827
Byzantine era

827–1061
Sicily under Arab rule

1061-91
Sicily is conquered by the Normans. A refined culture emerges

1282-1700
Sicily comes under the rule of the Spanish crown

1734-1860
The Neapolitan Bourbons rule the "Kingdom of Both Sicilies"

An active lifestyle with cycling and hiking has recently become the trend. Local groups put their new trekking shoes to the test in the *Riserva dello Zingaro* nature reserve, where their walks take them past abandoned tuna fisheries, swathes of yellow euphorbia and turquoise bays. Renovated farms attract Italians from the north tired of the rat race as well as other Europeans who are into organic living. *Nero d'Avola* has turned into the local cult wine, and top winemakers refine the taste by completing the maturation process in clay amphoras.

ADDIO MAFIA

The old image of the hard-done-by south, always seeing itself as the exploited victim with little to offer other than organised crime, a declining population and poverty, is a picture that no longer applies. Even the all-pervading Mafia has mutated into an economic driving force. Since the province of Palermo has been promoting its image at travel and tourism fairs with companies that refuse to pay the *pizzo* (protection money), the slogan "We are anti-Mafia" has boosted tourism.

SICILIA EST INSULA

This truism – "Sicily is an island" – drummed into the heads of Latin pupils conceals more than first meets the eye. The largest island in the Mediterranean is closer to Libya and Tunisia than to Milan. And it is too culturally important, too modern to pretend to be a mere provincial outpost. The Ancient Greeks performed their first improvised comedies in Syracuse while Italian matured into a literary language at the court of the Holy Roman Emperor Frederick II in Palermo.

1860
Conquest of Sicily by Garibaldi

From 1870
Wave of emigration to the US starts; ten years later the Mafia takes hold

1943–47
Separatists almost plunge Sicily into civil war

Since 1975
The Mafia blatantly terrorises the state and several spectacular arrests are made

Since 2011
Sicily has become Europe's front line for "boat people" refugees from North Africa

2022
Sicily registers its own national football team with CONIFA

Programmers in the Etna Valley have long since latched onto computer English and star chefs from Trapani jet back and forth to Tokyo to let the Japanese in on the secrets of the *cucina siciliana*.

Young Sicilians flirt quite openly with their *Eastern cultural heritage* – TV cookery shows enthuse about the Islamic roots of the *cassata*. The fishing centre and port of Mazara del Vallo would long since have stopped trading were it not for workers from Tunisia. However, the influx of war refugees and asylum seekers who attempt the dangerous crossing from North Africa continues to be a widely discussed issue throughout Europe.

BRIGHT AND MULTICULTURAL

Even without the controversial *ponte sullo stretto* (bridge over the Stretto di Messina between Messina and Reggio di Calabria), the Sicilians have been drawing ever closer to Europe. They have long become well integrated throughout mainland Italy as judges and poets, car mechanics and publicans, *carabinieri* and film directors.

And yet Sicily still sometimes seems like a continent unto itself, running at a different pace and according to different rules. Even the colours are different. Nowhere else are the cherry trees and prickly pears, the cucumbers and aubergines, as bright and shiny. In no other operatic performance is the public so vociferous as during *Cavalleria Rusticana*. Where else do children, dressed as nuns and monks, traipse along marking the Passion the evening before Good Friday? The Spanish and the Greeks, the Albanians and French, Normans and North Africans have all left their mark in the form of fortresses and cathedrals, sagas and culinary delights, music and facial features.

ONE ISLAND, MANY LANDSCAPES

The luxuriant purple cascades of bougainvillea, the spikey orange cactus fruit, and the silvery-grey olive and gnarled carob trees of the coastal regions provide a stark contrast to the sulphury, seemingly uninhabited countryside further inland with its waving fields of corn, overgrown paths and flocks of sheep in the *macchia*. The variety of beaches is also considerable, ranging from fine sand along the north coast, such as the one framing the fishing town of Cefalù, to pebbly lava beaches on the Aeolian island of Lipari. With blue grottoes below Taormina and the Gole dell'Alcantara volcanic gorge, all the delights of the south are concentrated on Sicily.

EYE CONTACT

Sicilians enjoy spending time with friends or engaging in conversation, and – like Andrea Camilleri's Inspector Montalbano – they love long, leisurely feasts. Extravagant tips, demonstrative idleness and tireless commentaries and appraisals with erotic undertones are eternal traits of the *sicilianità*.

AT A GLANCE

4,829,000
inhabitants

Wales: 3,170,000

98,000ha
wine-growing land (no. 1 in Italy) and 60 % of the Italian orange and lemon harvest

1,152km
coastline

Wales: 2,704km

25,711km^2
area

Wales: 20,779km^2

HIGHEST MOUNTAIN: ETNA
3,357m

Ben Nevis: 1,345m

WATER PURITY
7
Blue flags:
Santa Teresa di Riva, Tusa, Lipari, Ispica, Ragusa, Menfi, Pozzallo

YOUTH UNEMPLOYMENT
60.2%
in the province of Agrigento

7 UNESCO WORLD HERITAGE SITES

Temple of Agrigento, Villa Casale, Baroque Val di Noto (nine town centres), Syracuse, Arab-Norman Palermo, Lipari Islands, Mount Etna

10,000
producers registered make this Italy's leading organic region

MOST FAMOUS PEOPLE
Vincenzo Bellini (composer)
Lucky Luciano (Mafioso)

FIRST PAPER IN EUROPE :
PALERMO, AROUND 1070

UNDERSTAND SICILY

BURDENS OF THE PAST & HOPEFUL GREENS

Even travellers in the 18th century commented on the rubbish in Palermo. Since time immemorial Sicilians have treated the environment with a Mediterranean *laissez-faire* attitude. Industrial ruins, concrete eyesores and roadside fly-tipping are the downside of *bella Sicilia*. Recycling hasn't really caught on, and politicians seemed to have given up on the problem.

However, the Regional Agency for the Protection of the Environment (ARPA) campaigns in schools and boats patrol the coasts to make sure there is no illegal building work. While the regional parks and more than 70 nature reserves are visited by enthusiastic local hikers or *escursionisti*, the number of *bandiera blu* beaches (with a blue flag for ecological awareness) still has to be expanded.

FEASTING ORGANICALLY

Mangiare sano: the considerable value now placed on good-quality food has resulted in the sun-blessed island becoming Italy's biggest supplier of organic products. The younger generation is well aware of how post-industrial Sicily can benefit from an ecologically "green" image. Sicily has emerged as a stronghold of the slow-food movement, with an abundance of restaurants and eateries embracing the values of "good, clean, fair" and "traditional, regional", stipulated by *Osterie d'Italia*, the definitive guide to good food in Italy. The mass of fish in the markets seems to hide the fact that tuna is acutely endangered – something, however, that is more due to fleets of large, sea-going vessels than small Sicilian fishing boats.

SICILIA SANTA

Almost all Sicilians are Catholic. The Church still has a strong influence on virtually all aspects of everyday life. Most nursery schools and a lot of primary and secondary schools are in the hands of the Church, as are many social institutions. A white wedding and a church funeral are a matter of course; regular church attendance less so, even if the whole town are on their knees come saints' days.

COPPOLA

The *coppola*, or flat cap, now enjoys cult status and is a fashionable expression of *sicilianità*. Historically, in the countryside, men's choice of sun protection wasn't left to chance, as the type of head covering gave a good hint as to social status and origin. Tenant farmers, agricultural workers, peasants or shepherds wore the flat caps, while more sturdy hats with a wider brim were reserved for the rural and provincial bourgeoisie and the nobility. The *coppola* got a bad name through its association with the Mafia as it was largely worn by the big bosses' right-hand men. Now, Hollywood stars like Brad Pitt can be seen wearing a *coppola*.

HONOURABLE SOCIETY

The Mafia, the Godfathers and their killers have a hand in virtually everything that has to do with power and money. Drugs and prostitution, the smuggling of refugees and the extortion of protection money are just the openly criminal activities. A network of friendships with politicians and officials right up to the top opens up the path to big money for public contracts and subventions, creates minor posts and furthers major careers. The Mafia is a parallel state whose instruments of power include corruption, fear and murder. Whoever breaks the *omertà*, the pledge of secrecy, pays for it with their life. The internal power struggles are equally lethal, with most deaths coming from within the Mafia's own ranks whenever new bosses and families fight for their share.

The modern Mafia in major cities has long been operating on a global scale, networking both legal and criminal businesses, especially in the road construction and the food industries, in health care as well as in waste disposal. The annual turnover is estimated at up to 140 billion euros! Such capital is increasingly being invested in legal businesses, often in the form of hostile takeovers.

BRAVE ANTIMAFIOSI

Those who bravely stand up to the Mafia risk being killed. Murders are becoming increasingly brutal, not even stopping short of children. However, the success achieved in prosecuting the perpetrators and the severe sentences handed down,

Memorial demonstration for a Mafia victim judge Paolo Borsellino

combined with the solidarity and increased self-confidence of the general public, have weakened the Mafia. And instead of sitting in silence for the rest of their lives in prison, many of the "bosses" spill the beans. The 'Ndrangheta clans in Calabria have gained an altogether more brutal reputation than their relatively "civilised" counterparts in Sicily. This new image fits in with the island's political direction, created by the gay anti-mafia activist and left-wing politician Rosario Crocetta, who was voted to become president of the Sicilian region for the term 2012–17.

AN END TO PROTECTION MONEY

Confiscated property and the businesses of convicted bosses are made over to cooperatives; this provides a

Even grandma hurries to Taormina's intergenerational evening *passeggiata*

glimmer of hope in the fight against the Mafia, as well as helping to ease the state of permanent unemployment. These cooperatives produce pasta, oil, cheese and wine under the trademark Libera Terra *(liberaterra.it)*. The cooperatives themselves have joined forces with hoteliers, traders, farmers, craftsmen and builders – more than 1,000 in total – to form *AddioPizzo* and no longer pay protection money *(pizzo)*. A map with addresses of those involved – largely in the city and province of Palermo – is available at *addiopizzo.org*. For Catania see *addiopizzocatania.org*

INSIDER TIP
Don't fund the Mafia!

VOLCANOES & EARTHQUAKES

Geologically speaking, most of Sicily was part of Africa. Only the north is part of the Eurasian Plate, and is being pushed by the African Plate, which resulted in the formation of the mountain ranges in northern Sicily. Earthquakes are caused by tension and the sudden release of energy in the Earth's crust. In 1693, a quake destroyed the whole of southeastern Sicily. In 1783 and 1908, the most devastating earthquakes ever recorded in Europe almost entirely destroyed Messina; in 1968, a quake shook Gibellina in the west and 13 other towns in Belice Valley.

Volcanoes often appear along the seams where cracks and faults cause chambers of magma – which rise from the molten centre of the earth – to form. Etna and Stromboli are the two most visibly active volcanoes on Sicily. Volcanologists consider the islands of

Lipari, Vulcano, Panarea and Pantelleria to be still active, although their last eruptions were more than 100 years ago.

North of the Lipari Islands lies Europe's largest underwater volcano, Monte Marsili, which covers an area of more than 2,000km² and rises to a height of some 3,000m. It is surrounded by at least seven other active, underwater volcanoes and the Aeolian Islands. Marsili is permanently under volcanological surveillance, but it cannot be predicted if and when it will erupt or cause an undersea earthquake with a potentially devastating tsunami. In July 2019, Stromboli erupted killing one person.

STROLLING & FLIRTING

The *passeggiata* – the evening stroll – starts before the sun has set. Everyone seems to be on the move for the next two hours, when the main thoroughfare – the *corso* – as well as the main square – the *piazza* – are turned into a stage. People meet up and like to see and be seen by friends and anyone around. Gossip and news are exchanged and rumours spread. The *passeggiata* is also the perfect, carefully monitored occasion for lovers to show their affection for one another. Many an engagement and marriage finds their beginnings on the *passeggiata* and many business deals are struck there too.

SARACEN TOWERS

The massive *Saracen towers* are a feature of the Italian coastline and also of Sicily. In the ninth century, the

TRUE OR FALSE?

TRAFFIC CHAOS

Concertos of honking horns, dented Fiats, gesticulating drivers and the impossibility of parking in a maze of twisting alleyways. Many wouldn't even dream of venturing into Sicilian traffic. Certainly, Sicilians prefer to drive by instinct rather than by the rules. Feel free to edge your way through a red light, but remember to stop politely as soon as a pedestrian wants to cross the street (never at the crossing, though, of course). Once you've given your horn a good honk, patience is usually the order of the day, even in the wildest jungle of traffic jams. Go ahead, make clever use of gaps, change lanes at lightning speed; but pushy tailgaiting – no!

ISLAND POVERTY

Yes, youth unemployment is high, with many Sicilians slaving away instead in Milan or further away on the continent. But poverty stricken? Not by any means. Most of the city centres scrub up nicely. Instead of strolling around drab, affluent pedestrian zones as a slave to mass consumerism, make use of the advice given in small, independent, owner-managed shops. And the perennial elegance of the thousands of fashion boutiques testifies to the fact that Sicilians are experts at cutting a *bella figura*.

Saracens from North Africa arrived in their ships on the shores of all Christian countries around the Mediterranean, plundering and destroying coastal settlements and taking the local population back for the slave market. Well-fortified towns, however, were seldom attacked. The towers were within sight of each other and warnings were given by lighting fires or firing canons. This permanent feud lasted until the start of the 19th century; most of the surviving Saracen towers were Spanish fortresses from the 16th century, and many have been converted into hotels or discos.

(SIGN) LANGUAGE

Many young Sicilians speak good English. The majority of Sicilians speak standard Italian with clear pronunciation, even if the native *sicilianu* with its vowel centring and love of the vowels *u* and *i* is a challenge even for Italians. OK, *amuri = amore*, but who decided *beddu* means *bello* (beautiful) or *ranni grande* (big)?

Far more satisfying is learning to use a little native sign language: an index finger to the right corner of the mouth means: *This tastes delicious!*, while a curt nod accompanied by a brief click of the tongue is a clear "no". But best leave any cheek pinching for staff or subordinates to the Mafia bosses!'

L'ISOLA DELLA MUSICA

Sounds reverberate around this island, ranging from the clanking of Easter procession brass bands to the *verismo* opera *Cavalleria Rusticana* (known even to implacable opera haters thanks to the film *Godfather III*) or even a *siciliano* in E-flat major from Johann Sebastian Bach. On the island where the singer Caruso made his name, the young generation is frantically discovering the island's folkloric heritage, mixed with jazz or Latin American influences. In particular, the melancholic fado-influenced songs by Rosa Balistreri (1927–90) enjoy a cult following: the "Sicilian Edith Piaf" grew up in the poorest conditions, which made her ballads so authentic. New Sicilian stars have now taken to the stage, such as the rapper Ciccio Elektro, songwriter Carmen Consoli, the rock legend Franco Battiato (1945–2021), the musician Luca Madonia, or Ivan Segreto, who specialises in lounge music in dialect. The *Indiegenofest (indiegenofest.it)* held in the province of Messina is a symbiosis of world music and the Sicilian music scene. And where else in Europe will you find so many hotels and night clubs with piano bars where real-life pianists perform live?

OFF WITH THEIR HEADS!

Heads roll, Saracens are split in two and princesses abducted. There's never a dull moment in Sicilian marionette theatres, the *Opera dei Pupi*, when Orlando or Rinaldo fight for the Cross or for Charlemagne, with action and passion being the order of the day. But even the *puparo*, the puppeteer, can get out of breath, as performing is hard physical work in these family-run businesses. The brightly coloured figures can be a good metre high. They are hand-carved and operated using iron rods. In the 1980s, this form of folk art was in danger of disappearing due to dwindling audiences. Now, however, even local school classes visit the shows. Palermo, Acireale and Syracuse are the principal centres on Sicily where shows are held (see p. 48, p. 63 and p. 84). In 2008, the *opera dei pupi* was designated by UNESCO as part of humanity's "oral and intangible heritage".

MEDITERRANEAN FATALITIES

From an EU perspective, Sicily, the island right at the heart of the Mediterranean, used to hold a border post perched on the edge of Europe. However, this has now changed. Tens of thousands of refugees, who make the perilous boat crossing from Libya and Tunisia to Europe, have seen this escape route become the subject of heavy political discussion. Not only desperate people from Africa, but also Syrian and Afghan refugees fleeing civil war, attempt to reach Lampedusa, which is located just 138km off the Tunisian coast, with the help of smugglers. The inflatable boats are often hopelessly overcrowded and conditions are miserable, causing the drowning of hundreds of travellers time and time again. Italian and Sicilian fishermen, as well as aid organisation *sea-watch.org*, who have been rescuing those stranded and in distress for years, feel abandoned by the EU. Lampedusa has witnessed a serious slump in tourism as a result of the refugee camps and the horrific possibility of drowned refugees being

washed ashore. It remains to be seen whether the EU plans for migrant processing centres in North Africa will help to curb the desperate flow of people towards Europe.

TRINACRIA

The *trinacaria* – a winged woman's head with the two serpents, from which three legs emerge – has been used as an emblem for Sicily since antiquity, symbolising the island's triangular shape and its three ancient provinces, as well as being a symbol of the sun and of fertility. Sicily's emblem can be seen everywhere – on postcards and souvenirs, on market stalls, fishing boats and lorries, on pub and shop signs, as a trademark of a brewery in Messina, on stamps, flags, internet sites and official letterheads.

Real rock singer: *cantautrice* Carmen Consoli

EATING
SHOPPING
SPORT

Take a seat, order a pizza and enjoy your holiday on Lipari!

EATING & DRINKING

Forget the picture you have of typical Italian food, of pizza and spaghetti bolognese. *Cucina Siciliana* is different and diverse. It's made up of the culinary delights enjoyed by the many foreign rulers who made the island their home over hundreds of years. It's the most varied regional cuisine you'll find in Italy!

MARKET CUISINE: WHAT ELSE?

Each part of the island has its own recipes. Fishermen and shepherds, farmers and farm workers from the great expanse of inland Sicily all have different ingredients to hand. And the food of the gentry is different again from that of the working people. But what they do have in common is a love of colour and imagaination, as well as an ability to combine sweet, savoury, hot and sour things quite daringly; these, in the hands of Sicilian

mammas, are magically turned into delicious dishes. Fresh durum wheat bread, usually sprinkled with sesame seeds in the eastern tradition, is never missing.

INSIDER TIP
Palermo is loud and lavish

The ingredients are as seasonal as the displays at Ballarò, Palermo's open-air market: daily fresh fish and every vegetable imaginable from the home of fertility goddess Demeter, with wild fennel, mint and basil for seasoning, together with sea salt, olive oil and the freshly squeezed juice of local *limoni*.

DON'T COME TOO EARLY!

Sicilians love eating, especially in a restaurant or Sunday picnics on the beach; and they eat late, both at lunchtime and in the evening. If you can't wait, try something fried, such as rice balls – *arancini* – or chickpea fritters – *panelli*; they will soon fill you up.

26

Arancine (left) are certainly delicious, but leave room for a *granita* (right)

ANTIPASTI SICILIAN STYLE

Unless you order antipasti, you'll miss out on the best vegetarian food. Vegetables tend to be more of a starter than a filling side dish and are eaten lukewarm to cold. On the coast, you can also choose from octopus salad, tuna carpaccio, marinated sardines or deep-fried mini meatballs made from freshly hatched glass eels. Up in the mountains, you should start your meal with air-dried salami and pecorino – in Sicily, cheese is never a dessert!

PASTA & FISH COUSCOUS

The first course is almost always a pasta dish using pasta made from durum wheat flour without egg. Putting away over 100kg per head per year, Sicilians hold the record as Italy's biggest pasta fans. Twisted *busiate* and rolled *maccheroni* are firm favourites. Especially tasty is alla carrettiera

seasoning made with parsley, garlic, peperoncino and olive oil. Or you can enjoy countless variations of *sugo* with aubergines, pistachios or tuna. Risotto is almost always *alla pescatora* (with seafood). *Cuscus alla trapanese*, the steamed wheat semolina dish, is of North African origin and is served with a spicy fish soup.

SECONDO PIATTO

Although the *secondo piatto* is the main course, it tends to be on the lean side. Sumptuous pasta dishes are often followed by a delicate slice of fish or meat with a dash of olive oil and a wedge of lemon. That said, the red mullet, swordfish and calamari are usually freshly caught and come at a price: any good restaurant will show you the *pesce* raw – it's up to you to choose. You'll be charged by the weight. A delicious option is *alla ghiotta* (with tomatoes, capers and

Delicious almond pastry:
merletti di mandorle

cooling agent and was taken to the towns packed under masses of straw and kept in caves and cellars. The *granita* is a summer treat: watery ice mixed with lemon juice, mulberry pulp, almond milk or espresso.

herbs). Inland, the cuisine is dominated by lamb, rabbit, chicken and the coarse Sicilian sausage, the *salsiccia* (made with fennel seeds). Side dishes more adventurous than salad are rare.

DOLCI & GELATO

Sicilians often like to round off the meal with a dessert, normally with fruit of the season such as the exquisite blood oranges. On more special occasions, a *dolce* is served, such as a light almond confection with candied oranges, creamy tarts soaked in liqueur or cannoli rolls filled with sheep's curd. A showstopper with an Arabic past is iced *cassata* made from flavoured ricotta and decorated with candied fruit.

The hot volcanic island also sees itself as the inventor of ice cream: after all, the snow on Etna was a natural

COUNTRY WINE & DESIGNER DROPS

Sicily's wines have conquered the global market. Since wine growers have started harvesting grapes earlier, they have been able to produce lighter wines in keeping with the current market. Dessert wines such as Marsala and Malvasia are reserved for connoisseurs.

In terms of wine, the island is divided into two: red wines dominate the eastern half and the Nero d'Avola grape is a current favourite. Up-and-coming wine-producing areas are located around Vittoria in the southeast. On Etna, winemakers are experimenting with their fashionable orange wines. The western half of the island is definitely a *vino bianco* region. Dry grape varieties, such as Grillo and Cataratto, are an exciting option.

Apart from wine, the most important drink for the Sicilians is mineral water. Almond milk *(latte di mandorla)* and freshly pressed orange or lemon juice *(spremuta)* are also delicious. And at any time Sicilians are happy to join friends at a bar for a quick *caffè espresso*, which is widely regarded as a full breakfast. In the afternoon, you can enjoy a glass of Amaro Averna, neat, of course, without ice or lemon.

TODAY'S SPECIALS

Antipasti

INSALATA DI ARANCE
Fresh oranges with mild onions

ALICI MARINATE
Marinated anchovies with fresh mint

CAPONATA
Sweet-and-sour vegetables served cold:
aubergines, peppers, capers and olives
with a honey and vinegar dressing

PARMIGIANA DI MELANZANE
Aubergine gratin casserole with
mozzarella and tomatoes

Primi Piatti

MACCU DI FAVE
Broadbean purée with wild herbs

PASTA CON LE SARDE
Pasta with sardines, wild fennel, pine
nuts and raisins

PASTA AL PESTO TRAPANESE
Spaghetti with a finely blended cold
sauce made from tomatoes, almonds,
garlic and olive oil

MACCHERONI ALLA NORMA
Home-made pasta with aubergines,
tomato sauce, basil and salty ricotta

Secondi Piatti

ZUPPA DI PESCE
Catch of the day simmered in white
wine, tomato sauce and olive oil

TONNO ALLA CIPUTTADA
Tuna steaks with sweet, braised onions

INVOLTINI DI SPADA ALLA SICILIANA
Swordfish rolls stuffed with
breadcrumbs, pine nuts and raisins

BISTECCA ALLA PALERMITANA
Veal escalope in herby breadcrumbs
fried in olive oil

CONIGLIO AL AGRODOLCE
Sweet-and-sour braised rabbit

AGNELLO ALLA GRIGLIA
Grilled lamb chops

Dolci

CANNOLI
Tube-shaped pastry filled with ricotta

GELO DI MELONE
Watermelon jelly

SHOPPING

Majolica or marionettes? Sicilian crafts are back on trend, not least because young Sicilians like to combine local traditional style with modern interior design.

GET THE LEAFY LOOK
Fan palms grow in the far west of the island and their fronds are woven to make casual beach bags and sun hats. You'll find these in Scopello and San Vito lo Capo.

SICILY ON A PLATE
Gourmet souvenirs include elegantly packaged sea salt from the salt works of Trapani, expensive jars of sardines and tins of tuna fish, or mullet roe which is grated over pasta as dried *bottarga*. Europe's finest pistachios are farmed in the Mount Etna region of Bronte and are the perfect filling for white *torroncino* nougat. Kids, meanwhile, will be amazed by the deceptively realistic fruits made of marzipan *(martorana, pasta di mandorla)* from Catania or Taormina.

AN ALTERNATIVE TO PORCELAIN
Caltagirone and Sciacca are home to plenty of studios producing elaborate glazed majolica based on Arab and Spanish pieces – or individual interpretations of their ancient heritage. Equally, the roughly painted plates from Santo Stefano di Camastra have a definite charm.

BELLA FIGURA
To discover Sicilian design and fashion in the style of native fashion designer *Marella Ferrera (Piazza Cardinale Pappalardo 27 | Catania | marellaferrera.com)*, simply follow the local, style-conscious *signoras* to the elegant streets near the Via Etnea in Catania and around the Via Libertá in Palermo. And – although usually much more

Majolica-ware (left); mini tomatoes made from marzipan (right)

expensive – you can visit the boutiques in Taormina, Panarea and on Lipari. The markets are awash with cheap goods and fakes of brand names. Fashionistas can hunt for bargains from the half-Sicilian fashion label Dolce & Gabbana (Domenico Dolce comes from Madonie) at the *Sicilia Fashion Village* (see p. 66).

THE SCENT OF THE SOUTH

Zagara (orange blossom oil) and *bergamotto* give the citrusy base notes to many a world-famous label, from classic cologne to "Ortigia" from Syracuse and "Sicily" by Dolce & Gabbana. *Perfume shops* sell local perfumes with citrusy notes at low prices.

PUPPET KNIGHTS

Sicilian marionettes, made from wood and intricately painted, have long commanded collector's prices. But with a little luck, original *pupi* are sometimes to be found at the puppet theatres in Acireale, Monreale and Palermo.

PRECIOUS BLOOD RED JEWELS

Watch the coral carvers in Trapani fashion precious jewellery from old coral (the coral reefs have been entirely decimated). Hawkers on beaches sell trendy costume jewellery for something cheaper!

ISLAND RHYTHMS

Press pause on Spotify and pop on a freshly bought CD in your rental car. Taormina, Catania and Palermo all offer music lovers everything from clanging processional music to the latest Sicilian indie, including banned pirated copies! Or take a leaf out of the book of avant-garde bands or old local shepherds and buy a jaw harp *(marranzano)*.

INSIDER TIP
Plink, plunk, plink

SPORT & ACTIVITIES

Once an island for the idle, Sicily has quickly caught up when it comes to holidays for the active. It boasts a coastline of more than 1,000km, and the beaches offer everything from snorkelling to sunbathing. Sailors are gradually enjoying better infrastructure around the coast, while on terra firma, hikers, mountain bikers, horse riders and mountaineers can explore the island's mountainous centre and its magnificent Mediterranean flora.

CANYONING

The ice-cold basalt gorges of the Gola d'Alcantara, the canyons in the province of Syracuse and the streams in the Nebrodi and Madonie (Gole di Tiberio) mountains draw in visitors for climbing, rafting and river walks. *siciliaadventure.it*

DIVING

Ideal conditions for divers and snorkellers above rocky seabed can be found off the north coast or off the east coast around Etna. By far the best diving grounds are around the small islands. The waters around Ustica (hydrofoil from Palermo) are a nature reserve *(Riserva Marina di Ustica | tel 091 844 8124 | ampustica.it)*. Just as fascinating is the underwater world off Lampedusa, the neighbouring island of Linosa and around the Egadi and Aeolian Islands. Almost all islands have a well-established infrastructure for divers (diving courses, equipment for hire, cylinder service, decompression tanks).

GOLF

There are six golf courses on the island. Situated 10km to the east of Sciacca, the *Verdura Resort (Strada Statale 115/Km 131 | tel. 095 998 180 |*

Boots on for steam and sulphur: hikers on Vulcano

roccofortehotels.com) not only offers the ultimate golfing experience for serious golfers, it is an all-inclusive and highly exclusive design hotel with infinity pool and tennis courts, as well as three golf courses. In contrast, hobby-putters can try their hand at the nine-hole club of the *Villa Airoldi (Piazza Leoni 9 | tel. 091 543 534 golf-clubpalermo.com)* at the foot of Monte Pellegrino in the urban district of Palermo.

HIKING

Times are changing: it wasn't long ago that Sicilians looked down on the foreign "have-nots" who wandered around like farm workers in clumpy shoes. But young Sicilians have recently discovered the joys of trekking and *escursionismo* for themselves. The rugged mountains, wild upland plateaus with an abundance of flora and impressive gorges,

especially those in the southeast, require proper hiking shoes but the rewards are worth it! But at times you might need to rely on your scout's sense of direction and thorn-resistant trousers! The *trazzeri*, the old cattle routes, are overgrown and there are few maps marking footpaths for hikers and hardly any signposts.

INSIDER TIP
Take a compass and pocket knife

However, in the five large nature reserves – Etna, the River Alcantara, the Nebrodi, Madonie and Monti Sicani chains – you will be able to find your way easily and choose between hikes of varying degrees of difficulty *(parcoetna.ct.it | parcoalcantara.it | parcodeinebrodi.it | parcodellemadonie. it)*. Hardy hikers can stay overnight in one of the mountain huts *(rifugi)* run by the CAS (Club Alpino Siciliano).

Popular routes can be hiked in the *Riserva dello Zingaro* (see p. 96) as well as in the canyon-like *Cava d'Ispica* (see p. 69). The Aeolian Islands are hard work but a hiker's paradise, with steep climbs, lush *maquis* vegetation and breathtaking sea views.

You can take an online virtual pre-hike at *greenstontrek.com* and *artemisianet.it*

HORSE RIDING

Guided rides are available in the Madonie mountains. A favoured option is *Azienda Agrituristica Monaco di Mezzo (Petralia Sottana | tel. 093 467 3949 | monacodimezzo. com).* More addresses: *turismoequestre.com*

MOUNTAIN BIKING

An increasing number of mountain bikers can be seen on little-used side roads, tracks across farmland and through the forests on Sicily. The Giro route around Mount Etna, and the Madonie, Nebrodi and Peloritani mountains have challenging changes in altitude, often rising above 1,000m. It is less strenuous along the south coast, in the west and on the limestone plains around Syracuse and Ragusa.

A challenging tour leads along the *ridge of the Peloritani mountains* with divine panoramic views over the northernmost point of Sicily and the Stretto di Messina, which connects the Tyrrhenian and Ionian seas. Your camera will be poised time and again as you zoom from the Aspromonte mountains of Calabria to Mount Etna and the Aeolian Islands. The 95km tour starts in *Messina* at the *Portella di Rizzo* (466m), running along the ridge

(1,100–1,200m) to *Portella Mandrazzi* (1,125m), then twists through a series of hairpin bends to *Castroreale/ Milazzo or Taormina*. Good, up-to-date information (in English) is available at *on-sicily.com/cycling-in-sicily*

PARAGLIDING

This trendy sport is winning over more and more followers and there are now over 20 designated flying areas. For a particularly spectacular experience, you can glide from the cliff of Tindari. *Etna Fly (mobile 32 07 93 95 57 | parapendiosicilia.it).*

SAILING

The sailing tourism industry is less developed here than in the north of Italy. First-class sailing is possible between Tropea (Calabria), the Aeolian Islands and along the north coast from Tindari to Cefalù. Passing through the Strait of Messina, the *Stretto*, is an exciting but dangerous experience. This is a very demanding stretch of water due to the shallows, changing currents, sudden winds and the heavy shipping traffic. For an option with plenty of charm, you can sail along the lava-black "Cyclops Coast" along the slopes of Etna with numerous small fishing ports between Catania and Taormina.

TENNIS

Given the climate, tennis is not exactly top of every visitor's list, but many towns and seaside resorts do have clubs that are almost always happy to rent out courts to non-members. Open all year round are the six clay courts at

A window under water: the clear waters off Vulcano are ideal for snorkelling

the *Verdura Resort* (see p. 32), which even employs its own coach.

Sicily's most beautiful courts are located in Taormina's city park; the exclusive club is open to guests from some hotels, including the nearby *Villa Schuler (tel. 094 223 481 | hotelvillaschuler.com)*. You can even book coaching sessions in English

WINDSURFING

The best places to surf are on the west and south coasts as there is almost always sufficient wind: San Vito Lo Capo, Favignana, Torre Granitola and Triscina near Selinunte, Torre di Gaffe near Licata and Capo Passero in the southeast. Capo Orlando on the north coast is also popular among surfers.

WINTER SPORTS

A little eccentric, but definitely possible! The two winter sports areas on Sicily are Etna and the Madonie mountains where there are hotels, lifts and ski schools. At weekends when the weather is good, the resorts are very busy especially between January and March when you can be certain of snow.

On Mount Etna, above Nicolosi, 1,800m above sea level, is *Etna Sud*, the island's main winter sports centre, which has a number of lifts as well as cosy huts with open fires. In the Madonie mountains, almost everything is centred around *Piano Battaglia* (1,650m).

The tracks high up in the Nebrodi mountains are ideal for cross-country skiing. They are partly marked as the long-distance hiking path *Sentiero Italia*.

*Mare
Tirreno*

I. Ustica

Palermo

Trapani

THE NOR'

Isole
Egadi

THE SOUTHWEST p. 90

Canyons, dry walls and
playfully planned cities

*Mare

Mediterraneo*

I. di Pantelleria

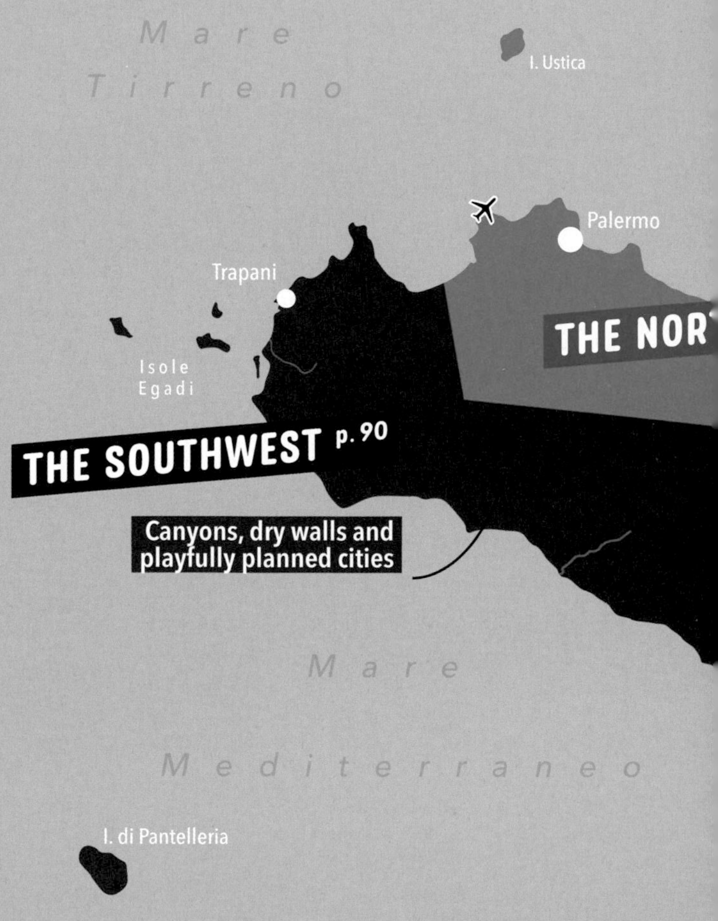

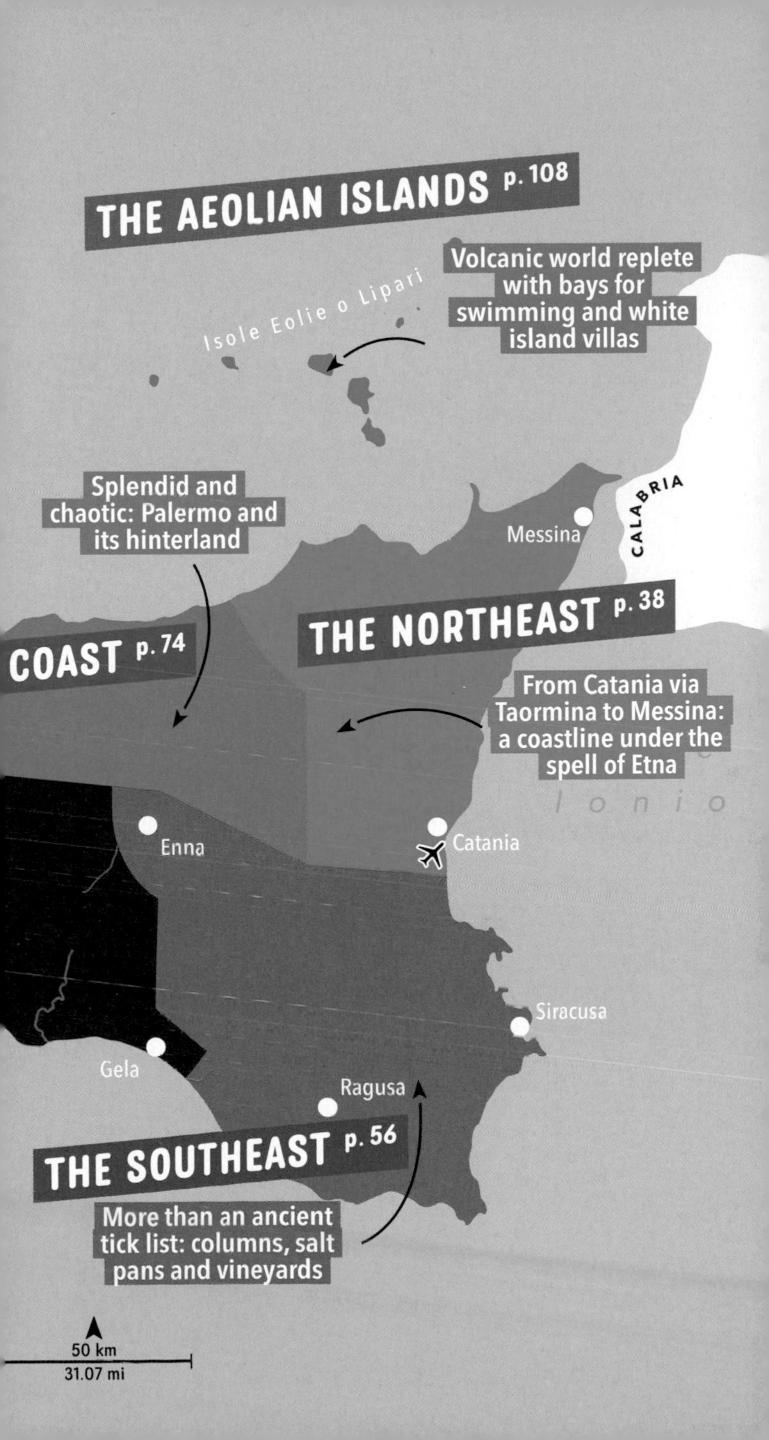

THE AEOLIAN ISLANDS p. 108

Volcanic world replete
with bays for
swimming and white
island villas

Isole Eolie o Lipari

CALABRIA

Splendid and
chaotic: Palermo and
its hinterland

Messina

THE NORTHEAST p. 38

COAST p. 74

From Catania via
Taormina to Messina:
a coastline under the
spell of Etna

I o n i o

Enna

✈ Catania

Siracusa

Gela

Ragusa

THE SOUTHEAST p. 56

More than an ancient
tick list: columns, salt
pans and vineyards

50 km
31.07 mi

THE NORTHEAST

UNDER THE SPELL OF ETNA

Visitors to Sicily are often pleasantly surprised to find such a lively place with quite as much Baroque architecture as Catania. The black façades of Sicily's oldest university city are home to ice-cream makers and boutiques, bookshops and laid-back bars.

Sometimes gloomy, sometimes capped with gleaming white snow, Mount Etna looms high above the city on the Ionian Sea. Despite the catastrophes caused by eruptions, its flanks are densely populated, and blood oranges, peaches, mushrooms and vines all

Greek tragedies and Roman gladiator fights: Taormina's ancient theatre

flourish here. Recent years have seen Mongibello (as Etna is known locally) develop a range of activities for holidaymakers, while a string of fishing villages stretches along the coast one after the other.

The hill town of Taormina attracts visitors from all over the world with picturesque alleys and nearby beaches. To the north, the remote Peloritani mountains rise towards Messina, the port city that is the gateway to the Calabrian mainland, while Milazzo on the north coast is the ferry port to the Lipari Islands.

THE NORTHEAST

Mare Tirreno

Golfo di Patti

Capo d'Orlando

Brolo

San Giorgio

Gioiosa Marea

Nasol

Patti

11 Tindari

Falc

Rocca di Capri Leone

A20

Castell'Umberto

Sant'Agata di Militello

Acquedolci

Ucria

SICILIA

10 San Fratello

Tortorici

Floresta

97km, 1 hr 20 mins

Nebrodi mountains

10

Santa Domenica Vittoria

Monti

Nebrodi

Ferrovia Circumetnea ★ 2

Passopiscia

Randazzo

Cesarò

Linguaglos
p. 49

Maletto

56km, 1½ hrs

Parco

Cerami

Bronte

Troina

Mount Etna ★ 1

dell'Etna

M

2 Ferrovia Circumetnea ★

Zafferana Etnea

Regalbuto

Agira

Nicolosi

Viagrand

Belpasso

Mascalucia

Catenanuova

Gravina di Catania

A1

Paternò

RA15

Carrubbo

Ferrovia Circumetnea ★

2

Raddusa

Giumarra

A19

Catania
p. 42

Golfo di Milazzo

Spartà
San Saba
Castanea delle Furie
Torre Faro
Scilla
Sant'Agata
A2
Villa San Giovanni
Calanna

Swimming beaches at Capo Milazzo
Milazzo p. 55
Villafranca Tirrena
Spadafora
A20
Stretto di Messina

86km, 1 hr 10 mins
Messina p. 53
Archi
A2racc

e dei ntoni
Olivarella
A20

Barcellona Pozzo di Gotto
Mili Marina
Reggio di Calabria
9

Mazzarrà Sant'Andrea
A18

ovara i Sicilia
Scaletta Zanclea
CALABRIA
Pellaro

Alì Terme
Motta San Giovanni

Roccalumera
Lazzàro

Savoca 8
Santa Teresa di Riva

ncavilla di Sicilia
7 **Gole dell' Alcantara** ★
Teatro Greco-Romano ★

Castelmola 5
Taormina p. 50
Isola Bella
Giardini-Naxos 6
Puerto Rico Beach Club

A18 Fiumefreddo di Sicilia

2 **Ferrovia Circumetnea** ★

Sant'Alfio
Riposto
Giarre
anta Venerina

San Cosimo

Acireale p. 47

ovanni la Punta
53km, 50 mins

Aci Castello

▲
N
10 km
6.22 mi

Fish market ★

MARCO POLO HIGHLIGHTS

★ **FISH MARKET IN CATANIA**
Swordfish meets fruit from Mount Etna
➤ p. 44

★ **MOUNT ETNA**
The mountain of mountains: the largest
active volcano in Europe ➤ p. 45

★ **FERROVIA CIRCUMETNEA**
Around Mount Etna on the narrow-
gauge railway ➤ p. 47

★ **TEATRO GRECO-ROMANO**
Taormina's dream view ➤ p. 50

★ **GOLE DELL'ALCANTARA**
Impressive river gorge with basalt walls
➤ p. 52

★ **TINDARI**
Wonderful view of Lipari ➤ p. 55

CATANIA

Villa Bellini
Savia
Via Umberto I
Via Salvatore Tomaselli
Via Androne
Via Sant'Euplio
Via Giuseppe Verdi
Via Giovanni Pacini
Via Lago di Nicito
Via Giordano Bruno
Via Roccaromana
Via Etnea
Via Plebiscito
Corso Sicilia
Via Giacomo Puccini
Via Antico Corso
Via Alessandro Manzoni
Via Santa Maddalena
Via Giovanni Di Prima
Via Caff
First
Via
Crociferi
Kitsch
Via Antonio di Sangiuliano
Via Crociferi
Via Gesuit
Teatro Bellini
Via Landolina
Via Quartarone
Via Teatro Greco
Via Etnea
Piazza
Duomo
Via Vittorio Emanuele II
Via Vittorio Emanuele II
Via San Gaetano
Fish market ★
Osteria Antica
Marina
Via Giuseppe Garibaldi
Via Transito
Via Auteri
Via San Calogero
Via Alcalà
Via Plebiscito
Via Cristoforo Colombo
Via Santa Maria dell'Aiuto
Camelot
Castello Ursino
Street Art Silos
Via Plebiscito
Via Grimaldi
200 m
219 yd

CATANIA

(□ K5) **Chaotic, volcanic, seductive – Catania has an enigmatic kind of charm. Sicily's second biggest city (pop. 311,000) is also known as La Nera, "the black city", and is under the spell of Mount Etna's powerful** presence. Its Old Town is also a World Heritage Site.

The architectonic ensemble of lava and basalt *palazzi* not only appeals to Baroque lovers – the city was completely redesigned by architects including Giambattista Vaccarini after the eruption of Etna in 1669 and the earthquake of 1693. The straight-as-a-

WHERE TO START?

Port: Parking spaces are few and far between so look for one near the port (Porto, Via/Piazza Alcala). From here, it's just a short walk to the cathedral and the fish market. City buses nos. 2–5 (night bus 431N) run to the city centre from the station. Long-distance coaches depart from the square in front of the station and the streets nearby.

die *Via Etnea* is lined with department stores selling fashion made in Sicily and ice-cream parlours serving the famous refreshing sorbet *granita*.

Catania, the university city with its North African climate, goes to bed late. The student crowd heads from the bars near *Castello Ursino* to the pubs around the *Teatro Bellini* opera house. An even more buzzing location is the city's morning market, just a few steps away from the cathedral, with its variety of colours, fruits, fish, noise and bustle, smells and aromas. This is the pulsating heart of Sicily!

SIGHTSEEING

PIAZZA DUOMO

Cathedral Square, lined with Baroque town palaces and with the black lava elephant, is the city's central hub, with the main shopping streets branching off it. The *Cattedrale di Sant'Agata* is dedicated to St Agatha, the patron saint of Catania, whose reliquary is housed here. A fresco in the sacristy depicts the eruption of Etna in 1669.

Head for the right aisle to find the tomb of Vincenzo Bellini (1801–35), the "Swan of Catania". The opera composer is considered a true master of the *bel canto*.

STREET ART SILOS

It's worth exploring the city's murals and graffiti: in 2015, artists armed with spray cans spruced up the harbour silos with Sicilian motifs. *Waterfront road SS114 opposite Via Flavio Gioia | short.travel/siz8 | ⏲ 1 hr incl. walk from the cathedral.*

INSIDER TIP
Look out for Odysseus in a suit!

CASTELLO URSINO ☂

The castle, constructed of black blocks of lava and with four massive corner towers, is Catania's most distinctive medieval building. In 1669, it became surrounded by streams of lava. It now houses the *Museo Civico* with a picture gallery, views of Mount Etna and ambitious special exhibitions. *Daily 9am–7pm | Piazza Federico II di Svevia | admission 6–12 euros | ⏲ 1 hr.*

VIA CROCIFERI

This street of palaces and churches with hotspots of student nightlife runs parallel to the Via Etnea, passing villas surrounded by small parks, to the university.

VILLA BELLINI

The park in this district of 19th-century houses is named after the composer of opera Vincenzo Bellini. The well-kept garden contains busts of major Sicilian figures as well as a viewing hill with an Art Nouveau music pavilion and lawn clock.

EATING & DRINKING

Catania's cooking fuses seafood and swordfish dishes with colourful vegetable platters, pecorino cheese and mushrooms from Mount Etna. The city is famous for its *granita*, containing mulberries, lime juice or almond milk cooled with water ice.

CAMELOT

The student crowd love to eat at the long tables here. Carnivorous young academics devour huge horsemeat steaks, while their vegan companions have no complaints at the antipasto buffet. 🐗 🏳 Horse meatballs for 2 euros are a firm favourite. *Evenings daily, Sat/Sun also lunchtime | Piazza Federico di Svevia 73 | tel. 095 723 2103 | ristorantecamelotcatania.it | €–€€*

KITSCH

Aperitifs, cocktails and colourful Sicilian food in a street of oleander trees. *Wed–Mon | Via Antonino di S. Giuliano 286 | tel. 095 286 5503 | FB: kitschbistrot | €€*

OSTERIA ANTICA MARINA

In the heart of the *pescheria* district where the morning market thrives. Seafood prepared in a variety of ways, even Japanese-style. *Thu–Tue | Via Pardo 29 | tel. 095 348 197 | €€–€€€*

SAVIA

The place to go for granita lovers since 1897. Opt for an almond *granita* topped with a little *caffè*. Also sells quick bites as well as simple lunch options. *Tue–Sun | Via Etnea 300/302/304 | tel. 095 322 335 | savia.it | €–€€*

INSIDER TIP
Where the Catanese enjoy their gelato

SHOPPING

You should definitely find time for a stroll through Catania's ⭐ 🏳 *fish market* at the *Porta Uzeda* in the *pescheria* district. It is Sicily's liveliest and most beautiful market. It doesn't just sell fish never before seen, but also farmhouse cheese with peppercorns, and all the fruits of Mount Etna: cherries, yellow peaches, blood oranges and wild strawberries. Beware: while you're distracted by the colours, smells and sounds, pickpockets may strike.

NIGHTLIFE

FIRST

Urban gardening, vibrant furniture, craft beers, graffiti and an olive tree in the redlight district of S. Berillo. A hotspot for local partygoers. *Daily 6pm–1am | Piazza delle Belle*

TEATRO BELLINI ☂

The interior of this magnificent building boasts ornate plasterwork, gold, red velvet and an extensive collection of historical paintings. It was inaugurated in 1890 with Bellini's opera *Norma* and is still one of Italy's top stages. *Opera season mostly Oct–May | Via Giuseppe Perrotta | teatromassimo bellini.it*

AROUND CATANIA

1 MOUNT ETNA ★
33km / 1 hr by car to Rifugio Sapienza

Europe's tallest active volcano towers north of Catania. Mount Etna (3,357m) can even be seen from the west coast of Sicily and Calabria on a clear day. Seen from the side facing inland, it is a yellowy, scorched, bald giant. It only turns a light green in spring when the grass grows. Its snowy cap doesn't always melt completely, even in summer. The best places from which to start exploring Etna's south side are *Nicolosi*, *Trecastagni* and *Zafferana Etnea*, from where it is only about 20km to *Rifugio Sapienza* (1,881m). This is where the tarmac road ends and the AST buses from Catania and Nicolosi stop *(depart from Catania/station square daily 8.15am, return from Rifugio daily 4.30pm; travel time 2 hrs | aziendsicilianatrasporti.it).*

Rifugio Sapienza (rifugiosapienza. com) is a simple hotel at an altitude of 2,500m. This is where the cable car *(daily 9am–4pm, last ascent 3.30pm, in winter 4pm, in summer late rides at sunset Mon, Tue, Thu at 5.30pm by prior arrangement | tel. 095 914 141 | funiviaetna.com)* leaves from. The slopes are open to the public.

Off-road minibuses can take you further up the track as far as *Torre del Filosofo* (2,919m). A return journey with a guide costs around 65 euros. Just getting to the top station (approx. 30 euros) is rather disappointing in terms of scenery. Plan at least three hours for the whole trip.

Guides for the summit can be booked at the cable car base station. Unguided tours are only allowed as far

Loud, colourful and beautiful: Porta Uzeda's fish market also sells excellent poultry

When Mount Etna erupts, the lava flow can be as hot as 1,500°C

as Torre del Filosofo and can be dangerous, especially when there is volcanic activity or when fog suddenly descends (there is no waymarked route). The temperature of molten lava is 800–1,500°C! Volcanic bombs are projected at supersonic speeds and can weigh up to more than a tonne. Close-up photos are best taken using a telephoto lens. The cordoned-off areas are for the protection of visitors' lives.

The eruptions in December 2015 were the most powerful for decades. In March 2017 and Christmas 2018, air traffic had to be interrupted because of ash particles in the air. In 2017, a hiking group at 2,700m were injured by fragments of rock thrown into the air, while February 2022 saw Etna spew out a 12,000m-high (harmless) column of ash. Up-to-date information about the Etna region can be found at *ct.ingv.it, etnaexperience.com* and *etna trekking.com.*

Piano Provenzana is another main starting point for tours to the top of the volcano and for 👥 🚩 donkey trekking, which is great fun for kids. Salvo and Santino offer a wide range of options, from

INSIDER TIP
Donkey rides

a petting trip to a winter ride in the snow: *Etna Donkey Trekking (etna donkeytrekking.com)*. Information is available from the *Mountain Guides' Office in Nicolosi (tel. 095 797 1455 | etnaguide.eu)* or in *Linguaglossa (tel. 095 777 4502 | guidetnanord.com)*. Choose from one of the tailor-made mountain tours organised by geologists Marco and Fabrizio: *Etna Moving (Via G. Mameli 54 | Mascalucia | mobile tel. 377 980 4142 | etna moving.com)*. Winter clothing and hiking boots are essential. Head out early – the summit is often in cloud later in the day. The hiking season is from mid-May until the end of October.

On your way to the summit you will pass recent lava fields that have smothered woods, fields and gardens. After just a few years the surface of lava turns from a dark black to a matte grey and the first pioneer plants start to take hold. After 20 years, gorse spreads rapidly. In the early summer, the sea of yellow is the most dominant colour on the slopes of the volcano with its black earth. Forests, mostly of mountain pine and sweet chestnut, prevail above 1,000m. Above 1,800m, only low-growing shrubs and herbal plants can survive in this volcanic desert.

Nicolosi is the starting point for excursions from the south. Just 1km above it there are waymarked walks to the *Pineta Monti Rossi* (the crater created in 1669). For information on the state of roads, the cable car, shelters and guided hikes: *Servizio Turistico Regionale (Via Martiri d'Ungheria 36–38 | tel. 095 911 505)*. Offices of the *Etna Nature Park: Via del Convento 45 | tel. 095 821 111 | parcoetna.it | ⬜ K4*

2 FERROVIA CIRCUMETNEA ★
Route 111km / 3 hrs 15 mins
A train ride around Sicily's mighty "ruler": the narrow-gauge railway rattles and shakes its way round lots of bends on its way through the barren landscape on the western flank of Mount Etna. Having reached the highest point, *Maletto (⬜ K4)*, it carries on past *Randazzo (⬜ K4)* through a black-lava desert before dropping down to the coast through a fertile area of gardens and vineyards. The journey *(never on Sundays)* from *Catania Borgo* to *Randazzo* takes two hours; it is another 75 minutes from there to *Giarre (⬜ K5)*, from where there are connections to Catania and Messina

(circumetnea.it). Or take a virtual tour at *swisseduc.ch/stromboli/etna*

In Randazzo it is worth visiting the Norman cathedral and taking a walk through the Old Town, which is built entirely of black volcanic rock. Gourmets should not miss 🐖 🚩 *Macelleria Spartá (Via Umberto 89)* where Nunzio

sells Bronte pistachios, sheep's milk cheese marinated in fig juice and salami from the black Nebrodi pigs.

ACIREALE

(⬜ K5) **Acireale (pop. 52,000), together with its neighbouring villages, lies on an elevated lava terrace above the Ionian Sea, embedded among countless lemon groves whose green leafy roof is overshadowed by tall palm trees.**

The Baroque town owes its wealth to the lemon trade and the medicinal springs that have been used since antiquity. Impressive façades line the main streets and squares. Experience life in the city on one of the three main interconnecting squares and enjoy looking at the town hall, the cathedral and the Baroque churches. A pretty street market can be visited in the mornings in the streets behind.

EATING & DRINKING

LA GROTTA
Cult fish restaurant in a lava cave in Santa Maria La Scala. *Wed–Thu | Via*

Acireale: a quick chat on the Piazza Duomo

*Scalo Grande 46 | tel. 095 764 8153 |
ristorantelagrotta.info | €€–€€€*

BEACHES

Most beaches are of the pebbly or rocky variety with only a few sandy stretches. The main places for swimming are the fishing villages *Santa Tecla* and *Santa Maria La Scala*.

NIGHTLIFE

The traditional 🎭🚩 puppet theatre in Acireale has a long history. The Grasso family puts on a great spectacle at its Opera dei Pupi Turi Grasso: *July–Sept, Thu, Sun 9pm and for*

INSIDER TIP
Where puppet knights wage war

groups by reservation. Or take a look in their museum *Wed, Sat, Sun 9am–noon and 6–9pm; winter 3–6pm | Donation suggested | Via Nazionale per Catania | tel. 095 764 8035 | opera-deipupi.com*

AROUND ACIREALE

❸ SANT'ALFIO
25km / 45 mins by car
This village on Mount Etna is well known for its cherries. Sicily's largest and oldest tree, the *Centocavalli*, a sweet chestnut estimated to be 2,000 years old, can be found on the road to Milo. Nearby, you can eat well in the restaurant at the *Azienda Agrituristica Cirasella (tel. 095 968 000 | cirasella etna.it | €)* where they practice organic farming, while mountain bikers dine in the shade of tall trees. 📖 K4

❹ ZAFFERANA ETNEA
27km / 45 mins by car
Below the awe-inspiring volcanic Valle del Bove lies this village, surrounded by gardens and chestnut woods. *Caffè Donna Peppina* on the central Piazza Umberto is well known for its *dolci* and delicious almond pastries. If you prefer something more substantial try the puff pastry filled with cheese, anchovies or olives.

Six kilometres north, the piazza at *Milo* boasts spectacular ocean views. The cosy 4 Archi *(Thu–Tue evenings, Sat/Sun also at lunchtime | Via Crispi 9*

| *Milo | tel. 095 955 566 | 4archi.it |
€–€€)*, meanwhile, serves 80 different
Etna wines and wood-fired pizzas
topped with local produce. *Ⅲ K5*

LINGUA GLOSSA

(Ⅲ K4) **The village of Linguaglossa
(pop. 5,400) lies amidst luxuriant
vineyards and hazelnut groves on a
lava flow. As in other villages
around Etna, Baroque architecture
dominates. The main church pos-
sesses a valuable altar made of
cherry wood. This is where the panoramic Mareneve route begins,
linking the north side of the volcano with the south.**

2002, this plateau with its hotels, cabins, cable car and forests was buried
under molten lava. The solidified black
lava flows are more than impressive.
Only the very experienced should
attempt to reach the summit on foot or
by mountain bike, having previously
contacted a local guide.

ETNALAND 👥
4D cinema, cable car ride and dino-
saur park – Etnaland offers fun for you
and the kids (theme park *Acquapark
open April–Sept*), at steep prices. *Daily
9.30am–6.30pm (entrance until 4pm),
April–June and Sept Sat/Sun, as well
as daily July/Aug also 7.30pm–1am |
admission 25–32 euros (cheaper
online), children under 1.40m tall
20–28 euros, children under 1m free |
Contrada Agnelleria | Belpasso | near
Paternò | etnaland.eu | Ⅲ K5*

EATING & DRINKING

AGRITURISMO L'ANTICA VIGNA
Organic winery on the road to
Trandazzo in Montelaguardia serves
home-made *maccheroni. 15km from
Linguaglossa | mobile tel. 349 402
2902 | anticavigna.it | €*

SPORT & ACTIVITIES

Piano Provenzana (Ⅲ K4), at an altitude of 1,810m, is the most important
winter sports arena on Mount Etna
and the starting point for 4×4 tours
towards the summit by *Etna Discovery
(tel. 095 780 7564 | etnadiscovery.it)*.
This is where the 20km *Mareneve* ("sea
and snow") route ends. In autumn

WELLNESS

ZASH
Full of contrasts from lava walls to
its ultra-smooth concrete pool.
Energising treatment or relaxing mas-
sage. Pick your own blood oranges
straight from the trees or enjoy your
met cuisine while sipping a glass of
the hotel's Nero d'Avola while enjoying amazing panoramic views with
the coastline in the
distance. Wine, art
and architecture har-
monise perfectly at
this Etna hideaway.
*Massage from 50 euros | Archi di
Riposto | Strada Provinciale 2/I-II n. 60
| tel. 095 782 8932 | zash.it*

INSIDER TIP
Water, wine and lava design

TAORMINA

(□ L4) **The best-known and most-visited holiday destination on Sicily, Taormina (pop. 11,000) is situated on a prominent hill at the end of the Peloritani mountain ridge high above the sea with an unforgettable view of Etna.**

The town centre is surrounded by villas and hotels dating from the 19th and 20th centuries. The picture of an enchanting medieval town unfurls to either side of the main shop-lined street, the *Corso Umberto*, between the town gates *Porta Messina* and *Porta Catania*, with castellated palaces, alleyways and small squares all linked by steps. The outskirts of Taormina suffer from excessive traffic; the centre, however, is an oasis. The *Piazza IX Aprile* halfway down the Corso is a meeting place at all times of day with its famous *Caffè Wunderbar* with the best view of Etna and the coast.

SIGHTSEEING

TEATRO GRECO-ROMANO ★

The most impressive view of the coastline and the huge snow-capped volcano can be enjoyed from the broken stage wall in the semicircle of this amphitheatre. It was hewn out of the stones in the third century BCE, in Hellenic times, when dramas and comedies were performed here in front of up to 20,000 spectators. In the second century BCE, the Romans converted it into an arena still seating more than 5,000 spectators. In the summer it serves as a backdrop for modern theatre and music performances. *May–Aug daily 9am–7pm, otherwise until approx. 1 hr before sunset | admission 10 euros | ⊙ 1 hr*

PALAZZO CORVAIA

This Catalan *palazzo* served as German headquarters for a time during World War II. The interior houses a folk museum (irregular opening times) and the tourist information office.

CATHEDRAL

The cathedral with its castellated façade dates from Norman times. The interior is plain. The *Baroque fountain* with the Centaur, Taormina's emblem, graces the square outside.

EATING & DRINKING

AL GIARDINO

Daniele Puglia and his mother run one of the last surviving family *trattorias* in Taormina near the city park. *Thu–Tue | Via Bagnoli Croci 84 | mobile tel. 339 300 1720 | algiardinonet | €*

DA CRISTINA 🐖

Taormina's snack bar near Piazza Duomo stays open until late at night selling delicious *focaccia*, *arancine* and grilled chicken. Since 2021 there's been a second, popular *branch (corner of Via di Giovanni/Via Iallia Bassa).* Daily | Via Strabone 2 | tel. 094 221 171 | rosticceriadacristina.it | €

OSTERIA NERO D'AVOLA

Home-picked mushrooms, orange wine from Etna and slow food. Unfortunately, the service can be slow too! Grab a table downstairs or outside. *Tue–Sun | Piazza San Domenico 2b | tel. 094 262 8874 | €€€*

SHOPPING

KERAMEION 🚩

None of the usual touristy ceramics are sold here, instead authentic art impressions of shoals of swordfish, orange gardens and Mount Etna on glazed mini tiles – a perfect souvenir. Sold in town at *Pigna a Pois (Corso Umberto 137 | pignaapois.it).* Head to nearby Giardini-Naxos for the actual

The view from Taormina's Teatro Greco-Romano stretches all the way to Mount Etna

ceramics studio *(Via Siracusa 17 | mobile tel. 339 207 9032).*

PASTICCERIA D'AMORE
A confectioner's wonderland which conjures up sugary delights such as lemon and pistachio marzipan in its tiny *laboratorio*. Pastries are served in pretty marionette boxes. Join Salvatore's cannoli class and learn to fill these famous ricotta tubes for yourself! *Cannoli cooking class 30 euros | Via Costatino Patricio 28 | pasticceria damore.it*

**INSIDER TIP
Sicilian-style baking**

BEACHES

The popular 🏖 *Isola Bella* and *Mazzarò* beaches have large pebbles. There's more room in *Letoianni* to the north, and *Capo Schisò* and *San Marco* to the south. The quickest way to get to Mazzarò and the SS114 road is by cable car. Buses to the beaches run frequently. A good cult option is the small 🏖 *Puerto Rico Beach Club (Via Nazionale 140 | Villagonia)* near the railway station where Samuele's beach bar is reached through a dark tunnel.

NIGHTLIFE

BAR DELL' HOTEL METROPOLE
Sip champagne on the hotel's splendid terrace with sea view. *Corso Umberto 154 | €€€*

AROUND TAORMINA

5 CASTELMOLA
5km / 15 mins by bus
This tiny mountain eyrie with its Etna views (ruins of the *castello*), almost vertically above Taormina, is reachable by bus. The village's old-fashioned sweet almond wine is its specialty. Handmade local lace, quite rightly, comes at a cost. 🗺 *L4*

6 GIARDINI-NAXOS
6km / 10 mins by bus
This tourist resort, famous for its beaches, is wedged in between main roads and the railway line. A walk along the beach promenade Lungomare is lovely. The shore area is particularly attractive near the *excavation site of Ancient Naxos*, the oldest Greek city on Sicily (735 BCE) with impressive megalithic stone walls. 🗺 *L4*

7 GOLE DELL'ALCANTARA ★
20km / 30 mins by car
West of Taormina, the River Alcantara and its waterfalls have cut a narrow gorge through the basalt up to 50m deep. The gorge can be accessed via steps from the road to *Francavilla* as well as by a lift *(7–13 euros, depending on the season)*. At the bottom, cool off in the cold mountain water, try your hand at bodyrafting (you can hire wellies and neoprene suits), or hike one of the signposted nature trails *(parcoalcantara.it)*. Swimming is also an option at the nearby 🏊 *Spray Park*

(mid-June–mid-Sept daily 10am–5pm | admission 11 euros, children 7 euros | golealcantara.it).

If you are hungry, you can enjoy local lamb dishes at the *Trattoria Rapisardi (daily | Via Roma 63 | Francavilla | tel. 094 298 1341 | €).* *K4*

8 SAVOCA

21km / 40 mins by car

You can see mummified corpses in the *Chiesa dei Cappuccini* in this mountain village in the Peloritani mountains. The Norman and Byzantine church *Pietro e Paolo*, which boasts Arabian intarsia work and steep-sided domes, is situated below Siculo near Scifi in a lemon grove of the *Fiumara d'Agrò* valley. *L4*

Basalt walls in the Alcantara Gorge

MESSINA

(L3) **For tourists coming by car or train from Calabria, Messina (pop. 222,000) is the gateway to Sicily.**

The ancient trading city, with its Art Nouveau centre, feels modern thanks to wide streets and boulevards and conspicuously low, but still impressive, buildings, which are considered to be earthquake-proof. But throughout Messina, there are few stones that have been standing since before 1908, when a terrible sea earthquake destroyed towns on both sides of the 3km *Stretto di Messina*, and claimed about 100,000 lives.

Today, the provincial capital is buzzing, especially in the main shopping street *Via San Martino*, the tree-lined *Piazza Cairoli* and *Via Garibaldi*. Slightly off the beaten track is the old heart of Messina around *Piazza Duomo* with the Staufer Cathedral and the Orion Fountain.

SIGHTSEEING

CATHEDRAL

Originally built in 1197 in the Norman style and rebuilt after the earthquake in 1908 and again after bombing in 1943, during World War II. The belfry contains an astronomical clock from Strasbourg (1933) and at noon every day it features a parade of figures including the city heroines Dina and Clarenza.

It's not just believers who make the journey here: the pilgrimage church of Tindari

SACRARIO DEL CRISTO RE

A panorama that has even inspired popes: enjoy a view of the harbour with the Marian column and the Calabrian mainland from the terrace in front of the neo-Baroque church (1937), dedicated to the victims of World War II.

MUSEO REGIONALE MUME ☂

The museum contains a picture gallery as well as displays of archaeological finds and majolica, among other things. The most valuable exponents include an altarpiece by the Sicilian master Antonello da Messina and two paintings by Caravaggio, who lived on Sicily in 1608/09 after escaping from a Maltese prison. *Tue–Sat 9.30am–3pm and Tue–Sun 4–9pm | on the Punta del Faro road | admission 8 euros | ⊙ 1½ hrs*

INSIDER TIP
A master of the Baroque

EATING & DRINKING

LA DURLINDANA
The courtyard of this excellent restaurant is a popular retreat for locals to enjoy fish *alla ghiotta* (in a caper and cherry tomato sauce). *Daily | Via Nicola Fabrizi 143–145 | tel. 090 641 3156 | ladurlindana.com | €€–€€€*

AROUND MESSINA

🟨 REGGIO DI CALABRIA

24km / 70 mins by ferry and car
Ferries *(carontetourist.it)* leave every 40 minutes for Villa San Giovanni on the mainland. From there, it's another 14km to Reggio di Calabria where the *Museo Archeologico Nazionale (Tue–Sun 9am–8pm | Piazza Giuseppe de*

Nava 26 | admission 8 euros | ⏱ 2 hrs) exhibits the extremely well-preserved Greek bronzes of naked bearded warriors, the *Bronzi di Riace* (cast in the fifth century BCE). These were discovered in 1972 by amateur divers. The bronze statues of young men are about 2m tall and weigh around 400kg each. The "Archaeology under Water" exhibition is quite fascinating! 🗺 M3

MILAZZO

(🗺 L3) **The town (pop. 31,000) is at the beginning of a small peninsula which has several good swimming beaches below the steep cliffs around Capo Milazzo.**

The pretty *Old Town*, located above the ferry port (for crossings to the Aeolian Islands and Naples), is surrounded by a massive 16th-century wall and dominated by the fortress of Frederick II of Hohenstaufen, which was later extended by the Spanish. Also worth seeing are the old cathedral (1608) and the church of San Papino (1629).

EATING & DRINKING

L'UGGHIULARU
Giuseppe Cannistra serves swordfish rolls, deep-fried red mullet, black squid spaghetti and pistachio truffle ice cream in the delightful courtyard. *Thu–Tue | Via Tonnara 36 | tel. 090 928 4384 | osterialugghiularu.it | €€*

AROUND MILAZZO

🔟 SAN FRATELLO & THE NEBRODI MOUNTAINS
95km / 80 mins by car to San Fratello
In Sant'Agata di Militello, the road over the pass forks off to *Cesarò* and leads into the heart of *Nebrodi Park (parcodeinebrodi.it)*. The 1,800m-high mountain range is covered in extensive grazing land and thick beech woods. *San Fratello* is a mountain village well known for horse breeding. 🗺 H–J3

🔢 TINDARI ★
35km / 40 mins by car
The cliff of Tindari is a north-coast landmark not to be missed. Below the 260m-high cliff face of the promontory, a sandbank enclosing a seawater lagoon and lakes stretches into the bay. The promontory is popular with paragliders! The Black Madonna in the magnificent *pilgrimage church* built in the 1950s attracts the faithful from all over Sicily. The sandbank and the Aeolian Islands can be seen from the square in front of the church. The plateau is the site of the *ancient city of Tyndaris (daily 9am to 1 hr before sunset | admission 6 euros | ⏱ 1 hr)* which has an amphitheatre, a basilica and the ruins of a city wall.

The organic *Agriturismo Santa Margherita estate (daily | Gioiosa Marea | tel. 094 139 703 | agriturismosanta margherita.com | €–€€)* has a garden overlooking the sea, restaurant, riding stables and mountain bikes. 🗺 K3

THE SOUTHEAST

BAROQUE IS KING!

The alleys of the ancient capital and port city of Syracuse ooze romance. The chic bars, however, are your first hint that the region draws on more than its cultural heritage for prosperity. The ancient Greek sites attract tourists, while agricultural exports and the petrochemical industry have created plenty of jobs.

The landscape inland is captivating – Sicilians often talk about the "island on the island". Rising behind the flat coastal plains with their dense plantations of almond trees and lemon groves are the Monti

Baroque architecture at the heart of Noto: San Nicolo (left) and San Salvatore (centre)

Iblei, which rise to almost 600m. In the mountains, barren grazing land, divided by miles of stone walls, stretches as far as the horizon. Here is a great spot to hike through canyons bursting with lush vegetation. The towns of Noto, Ragusa and Modica are like Baroque jewellery boxes, built in the light-coloured limestone of the area. Carnivalesque balcony supports adorned with mythical creatures are characteristic features of these towns, particularly those rebuilt after the devastating earthquake of 1693.

THE SOUTHEAST

Regalbuto

● **Enna**
p.65

3 Sicilia Fashion Village

Valguarnera
Caropepe

La Casa **4**
del Tè

Raddusa

5 Morgantina

Aidone

6 Piazza Armerina ★

Barrafranca

Ramacca

Mazzarino

Palagonia

San Michele di Ganzaria

Scordia

Caltagirone ★
p.64

Francofon

Grammichele

Niscemi

SICILIA

Vizzini

Buccheri **11**

Monterosso
Almo

Monti Iu

Gela

Chiaramonte
Gulfi

Golfo
di Gela

Acate

Vittoria

Comiso

Ragusa
p.71

Puntarazzi

14 Castello di
Donnafugata

15 Modica

Cava
d'Is

7

Scoglitti

Santa Croce
Camerina

Marina di Ragusa

16 Scicli

52 km, 1 hr 10 mins

Punta Secca

Zappulla

Donnalucata

Pozzallo

Cava d'Aliga

Po

10 km
6.22 mi

Marina di Modica

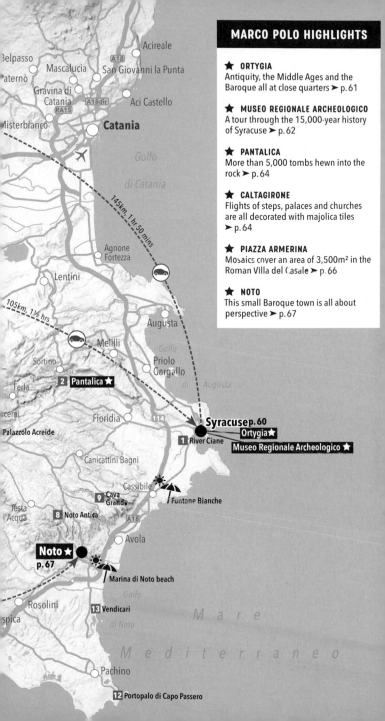

MARCO POLO HIGHLIGHTS

★ **ORTYGIA**
Antiquity, the Middle Ages and the Baroque all at close quarters ➤ p.61

★ **MUSEO REGIONALE ARCHEOLOGICO**
A tour through the 15,000-year history of Syracuse ➤ p.62

★ **PANTALICA**
More than 5,000 tombs hewn into the rock ➤ p.64

★ **CALTAGIRONE**
Flights of steps, palaces and churches are all decorated with majolica tiles ➤ p.64

★ **PIAZZA ARMERINA**
Mosaics cover an area of 3,500m² in the Roman Villa del Casale ➤ p.66

★ **NOTO**
This small Baroque town is all about perspective ➤ p.67

SYRACUSE

- San Giovanni Catacombs
- **Museo Regionale Archeologico** ★
- Parco Archeologico della Neapoli
- Viale Teocrito
- Santuario della Madonnina delle Lacrime
- Santa Lucia al Sepolcro
- Piazza della Vittoria
- Via Gorizia
- Piazza Santa Lucia
- Via Curma
- Via Trapani
- Riviera Dionisio il Grande
- Via dell'Unità d'Italia
- Via Torino
- Viale Paolo Orsi
- Corso Gelone
- Via Basento
- Via Francesco Crispi
- Via Luigi Cadorna
- Corso Timoleonte
- Via Piave
- Fontane Bianche
- Via Agatocle
- Viale Armando Diaz
- Via Elorina
- 'Golfo di Augusta
- Porto Piccolo
- Corso Umberto I
- Via Malta
- Golfo di Noto
- Via Trieste
- Museo Archimede e Leonardo
- Via Cavour
- Via Vittorio Veneto
- Scuola Alimentare
- Don Camillo
- Opera dei Pupi
- **Ortygia** ★
- Dom
- Via Roma
- Via Nizza
- 400 m
- 438 yd
- Osteria Sveva
- Passeggio Aretusa
- Galleria Regionale im Palazzo Bellomo
- Arethusa Quelle

SYRACUSE

(□□ L7) **In its heyday, this city was the creative hub of Ancient Greece, and comedy, the art of cooking, the ideal Platonic state and European Christianity all have their origins here.**

The safe natural harbour and the freshwater source of the mythological nymph Arethusa attracted colonists from Corinth from an early date. With a reputed population of half a million, this ancient city with its gigantic quarries was far bigger than it is today.

However today, the provincial capital of *Siracusa* (pop. 117,000) with its

Ortygia: Syracuse's station is on the outskirts of the city, but Blu1 operates a good bus service to the Old Town of Ortygia on the island. Rossa2 connects Ortygia with the excavation sites and the museum, bus 3 with the catacombs (all three in the modern city on the mainland). The Parcheggio Telete car park is in the north of the island.

fascinating monuments is fully on a par with its ancient rival. The historic centre with medieval lanes is situated on the "quail island" of *Ortygia*; a romantic district which has seen a recent revamp and now houses boutique hotels, Nova Regio restaurants and local fashion labels. In the evenings, young couples dress to the nines to meet for a sundowner on the Baroque Cathedral Square or in one of the bars along the seafront at *Lungomare Alfeo*. Amphitheatre-style entertainment can still be found at the *Opera dei Pupi* (see p. 63) when the marionettes are dancing or at the *Teatro Greco* (see p. 62) for performances of Ancient Greek tragedies.

SIGHTSEEING

ORTYGIA ★
The bridge from the mainland leads to *Piazza Pancali*, where the gigantic, dressed stones and columns of the *Temple of Apollo* (sixth century BCE) cannot be missed. In the morning, the square and the roads nearby leading

to *Porto Piccolo* – the fishing port – is a sea of market stalls and people. *Corso Matteotti* leads to *Piazza Archimede*, in the heart of the Old Town. Many stately palaces line the square and the promenade *Via Maestranza* that leads off it.

The magnificent *Piazza Duomo* with its mirror-smooth stone paving is dominated by the cathedral's massive Baroque façade that is subdivided by columns. The *Temple of Athena (Mon–Sat 8.30am–6.30pm, winter 9am–5.30pm | admission 2 euros)* from the fifth century BCE, converted into a church, lies behind it. The *Fountain of Arethusa* has its source below the promenade along the shore and gushes into a fishpond planted with papyrus. *Castello Maniace (Sun, Mon 8.30am–1.30pm, Tue–Sat 8.30am–6pm, summer until 7.30pm | admission 8 euros)*, the medieval fortress, offers wonderful views down the coast.

GALLERIA REGIONALE IN THE PALAZZO BELLOMO
A must-see gallery, and not just for believers: it's home to the *Annunciation*, a masterpiece by the early Renaissance painter, Antonello da Messina (1429/30–1479). *Tue–Sat 9am–7pm, Sun 9am–1.30pm | Via Capodieci 16 | admission 8 euros*

MUSEO ARCHIMEDE E LEONARDO 🎭🏃🎣
Battleships: real-life war games are on display at this museum showing how the mathematician Archimedes deployed cranes and concave mirrors in an attempt to defect the attacking Roman navy. However, all was in vain

Puppeteers at work in the Opera dei Pupi

SANTUARIO DELLA MADONNINA DELLE LACRIME

The plaster statue of the Virgin Mary, which cried tears in 1953 and has performed miracles ever since, is kept in a building with a diameter of 90m and a 76m-high conical roof ("lemon squeezer") that dominates the city. *Via del Santuario*

MUSEO REGIONALE ARCHEOLOGICO ★ ⚘

Sicily's largest museum contains spectacular prehistoric artefacts as well as finds from ancient Greek and Roman sites. Highlights include the Venus Landolina and an archaic kouros – a statue of a male youth – made of limestone. *Tue–Sat 9am–7pm, Sun 9am–2pm | Viale Teocrito 66 | admission 10 euros, combi ticket with the Parco Archeologico 18 euros | ⏱ 2 hrs*

as Syracuse was conquered in 212 BCE and Archimedes was killed by a marauding soldier. The war machines can be compared to the models

INSIDER TIP
Battle of the masterminds

by Leonardo da Vinci. *Daily 10.30am–7pm | Via Vicenzo Mirabella 31 | admission 7 euros, children 5 euros | ⏱ 1 hr*

SANTA LUCIA AL SEPOLCRO 🐖

This basilica is home to a true masterpiece: Caravaggio's altarpiece *Burial of Saint Lucia*, which has been returned to its place of origin *(daily 9am–12.45pm and 3.30–7pm | suggested donation)*. The neighbouring catacombs display early Christian wall paintings *(daily 9.30am–12.30pm and 2.30–5.30pm | admission 6 euros). Piazza Santa Lucia*

PARCO ARCHEOLOGICO DELLA NEAPOLI

A shady path from the entrance leads to the *Roman Amphitheatre*, largely hewn directly out of the rock face. Large public bull sacrifices were celebrated on the gigantic *Altar of Hieron* (198m long, 23m wide, third century BCE). The *Greek Theatre (Teatro Greco)*, with tiers also cut out of the rock, could seat more than 15,000 spectators. This is where the first comedies in Europe were performed in the fifth century BCE. It is still used for ☛ classical performances in summer *(indafondazione.org)*.

Latomia del Paradiso, the largest quarry in the ancient urban settlement, is now a cool and shady park with fig and citrus trees. The *Ear of*

Dionysius is another ancient quarry – 65m long and 23m high – which was carved out of the stone by slaves and prisoners of war. The unusual acoustics that make even whispers clearly audible provide the perfect spot to recite some classical poetry! *Daily 8.30am–6.30pm (winter until 4.30pm) | admission 13 euros, combi ticket with Museo Archeologico 18 euros | ⏱ 2 hrs*

SAN GIOVANNI CATACOMBS ☂

Syracuse was St Peter's first stop in Italy! The extensive early Christian catacombs can be accessed through San Giovanni church in modern Syracuse. *Daily 9.30am–12.30pm and 2.30–5.30pm (winter until 4.30pm, closed Sun) | admission 8 euros | ⏱ 1 hr*

EATING & DRINKING

DON CAMILLO

A wide selection of delicious seafood: choose the prawns with almond purée, broad beans with stockfish or the braised vegetable *bobbia. Closed Sun | Via Maestranza 96 | tel. 093 167 133 | ristorantedoncamillosiracusa.it | €€€*

OSTERIA SVEVA

The Spartan "Staufertrattoria" is just a few steps on from Castello Maniace. Orange salad and freshly caught fish at honest prices. Naive paintings and a pretty terrace. *Closed Wed in winter | Piazza Federico di Svevia 1 | tel. 093 124 663 | €€*

SCUOLA ALIMENTARE

Now this is what modern Sicilian regional cuisine looks like. The atmosphere is relaxed, the shelves full of non-mainstream wines, and the vegetables, cheese and salami from local organic producers. *Wed–Mon | Via della Maestranza 66 | tel. 093 109 5077 | €–€€*

BEACHES

Good sandy swimming beaches can be found in ⛱ *Fontane Bianche (〰 L7).*

NIGHTLIFE

PUPPET THEATRE ⚑ 🎭

Emancipated princesses and dragon slayers take to the

INSIDER TIP
Such drama!

stage at the delightful theatre run by the *Vaccaro-Mauceri families (admission 10 euros, children 3–12 years 6 euros | Via Giudecca 17/19 and 22)*, with performances held almost every day from March to October. Visitors can also see the intricate, handmade puppets in the *laboratorio* (workshop) and the museum *(March–Oct Mon–Sat 11am–1pm and 3–7pm (winter 3–5pm) | admission 2 or 3 euros | Piazza S. Giuseppe 33 | pupari.com*

AROUND SYRACUSE

🟦 RIVER CIANE

5km / 13 mins by car

This river, just 5km long, comes from two sources in the limestone hills and enters the sea near the former salt works in Syracuse. The sources and the upper reaches are the only places in Europe where  papyrus sedge occurs naturally. A 3km-long footpath along the riverbank starts at the source on the road from Syracuse to Canicattini. One-hour *motorboat trips (Vella family | mobile tel. 368 729 6040)* start at Anapo bridge on the Noto road. *K7*

2 PANTALICA ★

35km / 45 mins (Sortino) or 50km / 60 mins (Ferla) by car

A road runs from the villages of Sortino and Ferla to the necropolis created by the Sicel people. More than 5,000 burial chambers from the late Neolithic period and Bronze Age, dug into the rock, line the sides of the Anapo and neighbouring valleys. They were later used as a safe refuge during turbulent periods. Only one villa from the 11th century BCE has been excavated in the adjoining settlement. Hiking is also an option in the Anapo Valley as well as in Pantalica. *K7*

CALTAGIRONE

(H–J6) **The ceramics metropolis of ★ Caltagirone (pop. 37,000) with its church towers and domes can be seen from a long way away on a mountain peak.**

The streets are narrow and, apart from the famous *majolica staircase*, there are many other plain flights of steps. The grand 142-step staircase (1606), with its decorative glazed majolica ceramic tiles from 1954 onwards, connects the lower town with the *Palazzo della Corte Capitaniale*

142 tiled steps lead the way to Caltagirone's upper town

and with the principal church, *Santa Maria al Monte*. A walk through the well-kept, shady city park with its holm oaks is a real treat on a hot summer day. Next to the ceramics museum is a colourful Art Nouveau pavilion.

SIGHTSEEING

MUSEO DELLA CERAMICA 👕
Ceramics from antiquity to the present day and Sicilian majolica from the Renaissance and Baroque periods. *Mon–Fri 9am–6pm | Giardino Pubblico | admission 4 euros*

EATING & DRINKING

CORIA
Two small dining rooms near the majolica staircase and two chefs who like experimenting and who love fresh herbs and seafood. Try the sweet and sour stuffed rabbit or the orange salad. *Closed Sun evening and Mon | Via Infermeria 24 | tel. 093 326 596 | ristorantecoria.it | €€€*

POMARA
Rustic restaurant in neighbouring village *San Michele di Ganzaria* serving aromatic country cooking with big meat portions. *Daily | Via Vittorio Veneto 84 | tel. 093 397 8143 | hotel pomara.com | €€*

SHOPPING

CERAMICS 🏳
The decoration and glazing of expensive items like the classic Saracen head is carried out with meticulous precision. You can watch the craftsmen at work in their studios in the Old Town. Works are exhibited in the courtyard of the *Palazzo Corte Capitaniale* and in the shops in the *Galleria Sturzo*.

ENNA

(🗺 H5) **Provincial capital Enna (pop. 26,000), at more than 900m above sea level, is called the "belvedere of Sicily" due to its views over central Sicily and mountain village Calascibetta, and of Mount Etna and the mountains to the north.**

Well worth seeing are the fortifications from the Norman era and the Hohenstaufen dynasty, such as the *Castello di Lombardia* at the highest point of the town, as well as the octagonal tower, the *Torre di Federico II*, allegedly designed by Emperor Frederick II. The *cathedral* (from 1307) has an early Baroque wooden ceiling with angel heads symbolising the struggle between good and evil angels.

EATING & DRINKING

AL CARRETTINO
The perfect restaurant for a trip on Lake Pergusa, with a garden (fenced in). Cook Mamma Venera dishes up red potato gnocchi, grilled lamb and a cheese platter with coordinated chutneys. Her son Davide whips up gourmet pizzas from ancient Sicilian wheat varieties with crystallised basil. *Wed–Mon |*

INSIDER TIP
Choose from 45 varieties!

10km south in Pergusa | Viale dei Miti 13 | tel. 093 554 2021 | alcarrettino.it | €–€€

LA RUSTICA

Popular trattoria for business lunches: pasta with cauliflower, lentil soup and lamb offal. *Closed Sun | Via Gagliano Castelferrato | tel. 093 525 522 | €*

NIGHTLIFE

AL KENISA

If the Pope knew! An old deconsecrated Baroque church is now home to a *caffè letterario*, a literary café. Concerts in the evenings, cocktail and wine bar. *Tue–Sun 6pm–midnight | Via Roma 481 | FB: alkenisaenna*

AROUND ENNA

3 SICILIA FASHION VILLAGE

25km / 25 mins by car on the A19 Catania–Palermo, exit Dittaino

Right next to the motorway is Sicily's largest outlet centre with 120 clothes shops, bars, cafés and restaurants, all built to look like a small 18th-century Sicilian town. *Mon–Fri 10am–8pm, Sat/Sun 10am–9pm | siciliaoutlet village.it. ▥ J5*

4 LA CASA DEL TÈ 🍵 ☂

50km / 70 mins by car

Tea total: In Raddusa you can immerse yourself in an exotic world of precious aromas. The tea museum contains 600 different sorts and 500 teapots from all over the world. You can take part in a tea ceremony in the salon or enjoy the Asian-style confectionary and thereby support projects in developing countries. *Via Garibaldi 45 | donation suggested | booking required: mobile tel. 339 205 3677 | lacasadelte.it | € | ▥ J5*

5 MORGANTINA

34km / 45 mins by car

The ancient city is southeast of Enna on a mountain ridge with views of Etna and the sea. The wind and silence dominate the 2,000-year-old paved streets, the well-preserved amphitheatre and the huge terraced *agorà (daily 9am–7pm (winter until 2pm) | admission 6 euros | ⏱ 1 hr).*

Statues of gods from illicit excavations, previously at the Getty Museum in Los Angeles and since returned to Italy, are on show in the nearby town of *Aidone* at the Museo Archeologico *(daily 9am–7pm | admission 6 euros | ⏱ 1 hr). ▥ H6*

INSIDER TIP
Stolen gods

6 PIAZZA ARMERINA ⭐

32km / 35 mins by car

This town with its colourful church domes lies on a mountain ridge surrounded by eucalyptus groves, hazel woods and orchards. About 5km down a river valley, a turning leads to the UNESCO World Heritage Site of the 🏛 *Villa Romana del Casale (April–Oct daily 9am–7pm, Nov–March 9am–5pm (last admission 1 hr before) | admission 10 euros | villaromanadelcasale.it | ⏱ 2 hrs).* Back in the 1950s, the site caused an archaeological sensation when one of the largest mosaic cycles from the ancient world was discovered here under river mud. The techniques and motifs of the floor mosaics suggest the work of artists from North Africa. The villa was probably the hunting lodge of a Roman animal trader from the fourth century CE. The ground plan, under protective plexiglass structures, is clearly recognisable: public and private quarters, thermal baths, bed chambers, privy and the peristyle, the internal garden surrounded by a colonnade. Raised walkways lead to the "Chamber of the Maidens" with its famous mosaic of girls performing sports in bikini-like garments – visitors soon cause bottlenecks in their eagerness to see!

The *Agriturismo Bannata (SS 117, Km 41 | mobile tel. 328 298 8448 | agriturismobannata.it | €–€€)* is on the edge of a wood 6km north of Piazza. Art exhibitions and music events are held in the rooms, with natural stone and terracotta floors, modern furniture and antiques. Light food made to old recipes is served in the restaurant. Bread, biscuits, vegetables and wine are home-produced and organic. *Al Fogher (closed Sun evenings and Mon | Viale Conte Ruggero/Contrada Bellia | tel. 093 568 4123 | alfogher. sicilia.restaurant | €€€)*, which serves excellent, imaginative Sicilian food, is located on the road to Enna after the turning to Morgantina. *H6*

Baroque at its best: the balconies of the Palazzo Nicolaci-Villadorato in Noto

NOTO

(K7) **For a moment, you might think you are walking through the wings and onto the stage of an opera. The Baroque town of ★ Noto (pop. 24,000) is a UNESCO World Heritage Site thanks to its cohesive architecture.**

It is enthroned at the foot of the Hyblaean mountains above the coastal plain, with dense olive groves as shady as a forest. But this architectural fantasy was actually the result of a natural disaster: The medieval *Noto Antica* fell victim to the earthquake of 1693. The ruins can be seen 9km further inland. The town was then completely redesigned.

SIGHTSEEING

THE TOWN OF PALACES

The main churches, palaces, squares and open flights of steps can be found in the elegant district of Noto along the three parallel main thoroughfares. The central one, the *Corso Vittorio Emanuele*, finishes at the representative town gates and, halfway down, it opens onto the *Piazza Duomo* with a broad view of steps and façades. This is where the spiritual and worldly centres of power stand face to face: the *cathedral* and the *Palazzo Ducezio*.

PALAZZO NICOLACI-VILLADORATA

The monstruous figures supporting the balconies of the Palazzo Nicolaci-Villadorata are fascinating. Also interesting is the fact that parts of this 90-room palace are still inhabited by the original aristocratic family. Patterns made from flowers are laid out in *Via Nicolaci* for the Corpus Christi processions.

EATING & DRINKING

CAFFÈ COSTANZO ⚑

The almond ice cream or the mandarin and jasmine sorbet are more than worth the trip! *Via Spaventa 7*

Cava Grande: the Cassíbile river has created these wonderful pools

CROCIFISSO

TV chef Marco Baglieri promotes "zero km" cooking: all ingredients come from the nearest sources. *Closed Thu lunch and Sun evenings | Via Principe Umberto 46 | tel. 093 157 1151 | ristorantecrocifisso.it | €€*

AGRIMILO DONKEY BREEDING SANCTUARY

Onoterapia… what's that, you may ask? Quite simply donkey riding as a form of therapy for parents and great fun for kids. This *agriturismo* has seven breeds of donkey from the Apulian *asino gigante* to the Ragusa donkey for riding, stroking and admiring. *Contrada Piano Milo | Noto | mobile tel. 320 098 0424 | agrimilo.it*

Swimming and birdwatching are two options on the fine sandy beach in *Marina di Noto*; there's hiking and swimming in the *Vendicari* nature reserve, and swimming in the clean waters of the *Cava Grande* river *(Noto–Palazzolo road).*

AROUND NOTO

🔟 CAVA D'ISPICA
27km / 30 mins by car
The 14km-long karst gorge ends just below the Baroque town of *Ispica*

southwest of Noto. The main access to the gorge, which is home to some Byzantine grotto frescoes *(May–Oct daily 9am–6.30pm | 4 euros)* is on the road from Rosolini to Modica. The *Parco della Forza (May–Oct daily 9am–6.30pm | 2 euros)* in Ispica, with its cave churches, takes you an easy 3km into the gorge.

A culinary journey back in time awaits at the *Osteria Real (closed Sun and evenings | Via Calatafimi 13 | tel. 093 185 7604 | €)* in Rosolini. Almost nothing seems to have changed since 1959 at Signora Rosella's. *J–K8*

🔟 NOTO ANTICA
15km / 30 mins by car and on foot
Take the road in Noto to the *Convento della Scala*, an isolated Baroque pilgrimage church. Just 1km further on, park the car on the approach road to *Noto Antica*. The massive gateway and walls are the most impressive remains of this town destroyed in 1693. Here and there traces of walls can be seen above the weeds, including columns and church portals on the near end of the plateau. *K7*

🔟 CAVA GRANDE
20km / 30 mins by car
If you are in the mood for a refreshing swim and you're sure-footed, why not make a detour to Cava Grande? Take the road 287 then the by-road to Avola for 6km until you reach a car park where a steep, rocky path leads to a broad gorge. Further hiking paths lead along the crystal-clear river with waterfalls, lakes and sandbanks. Good shoes are needed to climb down into

the gorge 250m below, as the path can be slippery. Hiking poles are a good idea too. Officially, the path has been closed since 2014, but it nevertheless remains popular. At the weekends, there's a bar-pizzeria at the entrance. ▥ K7

⑩ PALAZZOLO ACREIDE
30km / 35 mins by car

Palazzolo Acreide dominates a hill, the highest point of which was the site occupied by the ancient town Akrai. Baroque craftsmen created an abundance of decorative elements, including faces and mythological figures, out of soft yellow limestone and wrought iron. The façades around the huge piazza are especially richly decorated. From here, a passage leads to the folk museum, *Casa Museo Antonino Uccello (closed until 2024 for restoration)*. Enjoy far-reaching views over the southeast of Sicily from the ancient *Acropolis (daily 8.30am–7.30pm | admission 4 euros | ⏱ 30 mins)* which has a small amphitheatre.

Regional food like chickpea salad with local truffles is served in spring in *Trattoria Andrea (closed Tue | Via G Judica 4 | tel. 093 188 1488 | €). | ▥ K7*

⑪ BUCCHERI
45km / 50 mins by car

Numerous *pale eoliche* (wind turbines) rotate in the hills around this winding village (pop. 1,900), which was rebuilt after the earthquake of 1693. Tucked away in the maze of alleyways, the quaint village trattoria Osteria U Locale *(closed Tue | Via*

Dusmet 14 | tel. 093 187 3923 | ulo-cale.com | €) will soon have your mouth watering with roast wild boar, tripe, almond casseroles, goat's cheese, mushrooms and handmade pasta. ▥ J7

⑫ PORTO PALO DI CAPO PASSERO
28km / 35 mins by car

This small town on Sicily's southernmost point, with its busy fishing port, has become a popular holiday destination thanks to the extensive dunes and beaches to the north near *Vendicari* and the sandy bays. Windsurfers come for the strong winds.

The terrace of the picturesque *Cialoma (daily | Piazza Regina Margherita 23 | tel. 093 184 1772 | €€)* in *Marzamemi*, the neighbouring fishing village that consists of a few flat-roofed stone huts, often serves as a location for Italian TV crews. ▥ K8

⑬ VENDICARI
13km / 15 mins by car

Vendicari Nature Reserve is synonymous with pure care-free relaxation. It incorporates wide sandy beaches, dunes with Mediterranean *macchia*, swamps and lagoons, which are a unique paradise for birds and a delight for birdwatchers. 250 different species of bird live here, including flamingos, storks, herons, ibis and spoonbills. *riserva-vendicari.it*

The *Villa Romana Tellaro (daily 9am–7pm | admission 6 euros | ⏱ 1 hr)* is on the Porto Palo road right next to the sea, at the north boundary of

Vendicari Nature Reserve. Late Roman mosaics of hunting scenes and heroic figures from the *Iliad* can now be viewed after 30 years of excavation. ⟐ *K8*

RAGUSA

(⟐ J7) **The Baroque jewel of Ragusa (pop. 73,000), fantastically towering above deep canyons, is the capital of the smallest and wealthiest province on Sicily. The oil fields, now fully exhausted, launched a short industrial boom around 1960.**

Ragusa has two centres: the more modern *Ragusa* with its wide streets, and the small Baroque *Ibla* of the nobility, clerics, craftspeople and agricultural workers, with its flights of steps, narrow alleyways and little squares where young people like to meet in the evening. The *Ecò-Bar (Via Rumor 40),* which Giuseppe Gurrieri created in an empty sports hall on the outskirts of the city, is widely seen as a shining example of contemporary architecture.

The novels in the *Commissario Montalbano* series were filmed for television in the little towns and coastal villages in this province. His house is in Puntasecca; Donnalucata is the port of the fictional town "Vigata". The Baroque setting of Ragusa Ibla, Scicli and Modica turned the series, based on the crime novels by Andrea Camilleri, into a visual delight.

High above the alleys of Ibla: the dome of Duomo di San Giorgio

SIGHTSEEING

DUOMO DI SAN GIORGIO
The main church in Ibla, with its imposing façade and flight of steps, is an exceptional example of the curving Baroque style in Sicily.

SAN GIORGIO VECCHIO
The ruins of a Norman church with a weathered portal. From the park behind you have a fantastic view of the town above and the gorge.

Oranges are transformed into tart yet sweet treats at the Dolceria Bonajuto in Modica

EATING & DRINKING

GELATI DIVINI

One of the most unusual ice-cream makers on the island with flavours such as carob bean, blood orange or Marsala. *Open daily in summer until 1am | Piazza Duomo 20 | Ragusa Ibla | gelatidivini.it*

I BANCHI

INSIDER TIP
Aristocratic cuisine goes casual

Bakery, Sicilian deli or osteria? It doesn't really matter. Star chef Ciccio Sultano spoils young trendsetters with delicious focaccia made from old varieties of wheat. *Daily | Via Orfanotrofio 39 | tel. 093 265 5000 | ibanchiragusa.it*

KONZA

A fashionable, modern-style haunt of locals, serving authentic *pizzoli* (pizza rolls). Slow service. *Closed lunchtime | Via Mariannina Coffa 9 | tel. 093 268 6561 | konza. it | €*

MAJORE

Restaurant in the centre of the neighbouring village Chiaramonte Gulfi (18km). Popular for organic stuffed pork chops since 1896. The animals are fattened with whey and carob. *Closed Mon and in July | Via Martiri Ungheresi 12 | tel. 093 292 8019 | majore.it | €*

SHOPPING

14 AGRITURISMO VILLA ZOTTOPERA

This 17th-century manor farm offers tastings and sales of its own organic oil, wine and vegetables. Cooking and baking classes will have you up to scratch and making *caponata* and *cassata* in no time. *8km towards Chiaramonte | mobile tel. 387 800 842 | villazottopera.it*

BEACHES

Scoglitti *(32km west | H7)* and Pozzallo *(40km southeast | J8)* are natural beaches with sand dunes.

AROUND RAGUSA

15 CASTELLO DI DONNAFUGATA

19km / 25 mins by car

Leopard dreams: this palace with park and labyrinth was redecorated in a neo-Moorish style in the 19th century, the interior decked out with mirrors, frescos and antique furniture *(daily 9am–7pm (winter until 4pm) | admission incl. park 6 euros | ⏲ 2 hrs).* Luchino Visconti was inspired to make his film *The Leopard* (1963) here. The *Trattoria Al Castello (closed Mon | tel. 093 261 9260 | alcastellodonnafugata. com | €)* which serves simple dishes is housed in the former stables. 📖 *J7*

🔟 MODICA

16km / 25 mins by car
The former capital (pop. 53,500) of the ancient county of Modica, identical to the present-day province of Ragusa, is located at the base of two karst gorges that meet at the central square. The Old Town, with its narrow alleyways and flights of steps, climbs the steep slopes, whereas the two main streets with their promenades, churches and palaces of the nobility run along the valley. The dominant architectural style here is also fancifully exuberant Baroque, fine examples of which are the main church, *San Pietro* in the lower town, and *San Giorgio* with five portals and a flight of 250 steps.

In the *Fattoria delle Torri (closed Tue | Vico Napolitano 14 | tel. 093 275 1286 | €€€)* in the middle of the Old Town, you can eat Sicilian nouvelle cuisine like tuna in sesame crust.

Modica is Sicily's earliest centre of the chocolate industry

– you have to try the dairy-free chilli chocolate made according to Spanish-Aztec recipes from the 16th century! The *Corso Umberto* is perfect for a chocolate

tour: for example the *Museo del Cioccolato (Mon–Sat, 10am–2pm and 4–7pm, Sun 10am–1pm | admission 3 euros | No. 149 | ⏲ 45 mins),* followed by *Antica Dolceria Bonajuto (No. 159)* and Quetzal, a *bottega solidale* in which Fairtrade products are processed. 📖 *J7*

🔟 SCICLI

27km / 40 mins by car
The Baroque town Scicli (pop. 27,000), which is only a few roads wide, winds its way down a gorge. You can get a good impression of its unusual worm-shaped location from the church of San Matteo, further up. Art historians consider the *Palazzo Beneventano* with its chubby grimacing faces to be one of the most imaginative Baroque buildings on the island. The di Tommasi family are experts in catering for refreshments: their unusually located underground *osteria La Grotta (closed Mon | Via Dolomiti 62 | tel. 093 293 1363 | lagrottascicli.it | €€)* serves up ray croquettes or pizza made from ancient varieties of wheat. 📖 *J8*

WHERE TO STAY IN MODICA

LEOPARD ROOM
Sleep like a Bourbon princess in the frescoed rooms of Palazzo Failla *(9 rooms | Modica | Via Blandini 5 | tel. 093 294 1059 | palazzofailla.it | €€–€€€)* and recreate scenes from cult film *The Leopard*.

THE
NORTH COAST

A city with a buzz, Palermo is both the capital and a lifestyle destination. The metropolis lazily stretches out at the foot of Monte Pellegrino in the "Golden Shell" *(Conca d'Oro).*

Sprawling suburbs have replaced the groves of blood oranges planted by Arabs in the ninth century, but the palm-adorned centre – in many parts ruined quite charmingly – offers a whistlestop tour through a thousand years of Mediterranean history: gold mosaics and Moorish domes, an emperor's tomb, Baroque

Long forgotten Cefalù has retained much of its medieval flair

fountains, Italy's largest opera house and street markets smelling of basil and street food.

Its tapestry of mosaics makes Monreale cathedral a tourist magnet. To the east, the rugged Madonie mountains rise behind the north coast. Rarely have rivers created plains whose lush green mandarin orchards contrast so strikingly with the karst mountain ranges that were once the perfect Mafia hideout. Another jewel is Cefalù with its sandy beach and Norman cathedral.

THE NORTH COAST

MARCO POLO HIGHLIGHTS

★ **PALAZZO DEI NORMANNI & CAPPELLA PALATINA**
Byzantines and Arabs created this royal palace ➤ p. 80

★ **PALERMO'S STREET MARKETS**
Colourful, loud and lively: an unmissable experience ➤ p. 84

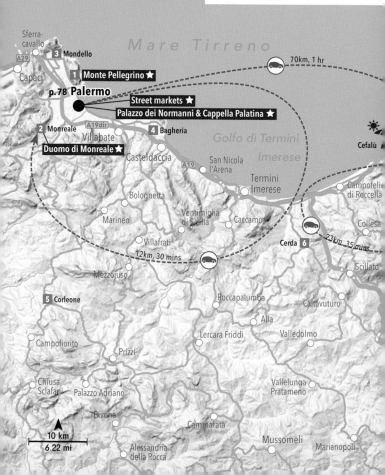

Mare Tirreno

Sferra-cavallo

A29

Capaci

3 Mondello

1 Monte Pellegrino ★

70km, 1 hr

p.78 **Palermo**

Street markets ★

Palazzo dei Normanni & Cappella Palatina ★

2 Monreale

A19dir

Villabate

4 Bagheria

Golfo di Termini

Duomo di Monreale ★

Casteldaccia

San Nicola l'Arena

Imerese

Cefalù

A19

Termini Imerese

Campofeli di Roccella

Bolognetta

Marinèo

Ventimiglia di Sicilia

Caccamo

Collesa

Cerda **6**

23km, 35 mins

Scillato

Villafrati

12km, 30 mins

Mezzojuso

5 Corleone

Roccapalumba

Caltavuturo

Campofiorito

Alia

Prizzi

Lercara Friddi

Valledolmo

Chiusa Sclafani

Palazzo Adriano

Vallelunga Pratameno

Bivona

Cammarata

Mussomeli

Marianopoli

10 km

6.22 mi

Alessandria della Rocca

★ **MONTE PELLEGRINO**
A bird's-eye view of all of Palermo ➤ p. 84

★ **DUOMO DI MONREALE**
This cathedral is one of the greatest
examples of Norman art ➤ p. 85

★ **DUOMO DI CEFALÙ**
The fortress-like place of worship can be
seen from afar ➤ p. 87

★ **LE MADONIE**
Beautiful wild scenery and forgotten
mountain villages ➤ p. 88

Jack's Beach
Capo d'Orlando **10**

Rocca di
Capri Leone

Sant'Agata
di Militello

Acquedolci

San Fratello

Duomo di Cefalù ★

Cefalù
p. 86

Finale

A20

9 Fiumara
d'Arte

Marina
di Caronia

Santo Stefano
di Camastra

ello

8 Castelbuono

Mistretta

Le Madonie ★

SICILIA

Cesarò

izzi Generosa

Petralia
Soprana

Gangi

Cerami

Troina

Nicosia

A19

Alimena

Villapriolo

Leonforte

Agira

Regalbuto

Villarosa

Calascibetta

Enna

A19

Catenanuova

PALERMO

Berlin Cafè
Piazza Luigi Sturzo
Via della Libertà
Via I La Lumia
Via Emerico Amari
Via Francesco Crispi
Via Principe di Scordia
Porto
Piazza Castelnuovo
Via Roma
Via Sant'Oliva
Via Ruggero Settimo
Piazza XIII Vittime
Via Camillo Benso Conte di Cavour
Museo Archeologico
Walking with The Leopard
La Zisa
Teatro Massimo
Mimmo Cuticchio
Tanto di Coppola
Fud
Via Valverde oratories & churches
La Cala
Via Volturno
Palermo Store
Piazza San Domenico
Via Bandiera
Mercato del Capo (Street market) ★
Via della Cala
Museo Inter delle Mario
Via
Beati Paoli
Via Judica
Via del Celso
Via Maqueda
I Lattarini ★ (Street market)
Via Vittorio Emanuele
Via Bottai
La Kalsa
Galleria Regio
Via Papireto
Via Merlo
Antica Focacceria S. Francesco
Via Matteo Bonello
Bisso Bistrot
La Martorana
Via Roma
Galleria d'Arte Moderna (GAM)
Cattedrale (Duomo)
Via Vittorio Emanuele
Pot Cucina & Bottega
Via Divisi
Convento dei Cappuccini
Teatro Argento
Mercato Ballarò (Street market) ★
Via Abramo Lincoln
Palazzo dei Normanni & Cappella Palatina ★
Via Albergheria
Corso dei Mille
San Giovanni degli Eremiti
Corso Tukory
Via Oreto
Palermo Centrale
Via Carlo Forlanini

PALERMO

(□ E3) **Maybe you're a fan of graffiti? Rubble aesthetics? Or start-ups in crumbling backyards? You'll find all this and more in Palermo (pop. 658,000), which is as hip as London but with better food, fashion and art.**

After the bombings of World War II and years of Mafia lethargy, Sicily's grandiose capital experienced a long period of neglect – those who could, moved to the modern city outskirts. Today, a new generation is determined to discover the charm of the Arabic-Baroque Old Town famous for its markets. The residents are working

Sicilia
Umberto I
Orto Botanico
Via Ponte di Mare
Via Tiro a Segno
Ecomuseo Mare
Memoria Viva

WHERE TO START?

Centre: Be warned, traffic will be chaotic! By car, simply follow signs to the harbour *(porto)* where you should find somewhere to park in the Via Crispi or in the roads behind (pay and display). Take the Via Crispi and you'll find yourself in the middle of Old Palermo around La Cala bay. From the station *(Stazione Centrale)*, which is also where most coaches stop, the Via Roma leads directly through the centre. Warning: the route to the airport is not well signposted!

The magnificence of the Norman buildings and mosaics stopped later generations from demolishing, remodelling or covering them up. There is nothing left from the Emirate era when hundreds of muezzins made the call to prayer at the mosques in what was the largest city in 10th-century Europe. Nevertheless, the Moorish domes of early Norman churches, such as *San Giovanni degli Eremiti* and *San Cataldo*, as well as the garden palace *La Zisa* give some impression of the Arabic influence in Sicily.

hard to renovate, without falling victim to gentrification. Boutiques, B&Bs and street-food stalls are springing up in Europe's 2018 Capital of Culture. *Movida* is now the order of the day: some streets are so crowded late into the night that you come to a standstill.

As everywhere in Sicily, the dominant architectural style is Baroque.

SIGHTSEEING

VIA VALVERDE ORATORIES & CHURCHES

Just a few yards apart, hidden behind the massive Baroque church of San Domenico, are a number of small churches and oratories. *Oratorio del*

Rosario and *Oratorio di Santa Cita* contain plasterwork figures by the Baroque artist Giacomo Serpotta; the churches *Santa Cita, Santa Maria in Valverde* and *San Giorgio dei Genovesi* are richly decorated with statues and stone intarsia work. *Daily 10am–6pm | admission 6 euros | ilgeniodipalermo. com| ⏱ 1½ hrs*

MUSEO ARCHEOLOGICO

The museum is housed in a former monastery. Burial stelae and sarcophagi are displayed in the Renaissance cloister. The ancient metopes (reliefs on a temple frieze) from Selinunt are exceptional examples of Greek sculpture. *Tue–Sat 9am–6pm, Sun 9am–1.30pm | Piazza Olivella 24 | admission 6 euros | ⏱ 1½ hrs*

TEATRO MASSIMO ☂

This theatre staged the première of Puccini's masterpiece *La Bohème*. A temple for fans of opera – 3,200 of them to be exact – and known among cinemagoers for the bloody finale of *Godfather III*. It was built in 1875–97 by the Palermo-born Giovan B. Basile. Inside, the *Caffè del Teatro (daily 10am–11pm)* is a hidden gem. *Opera season Nov–May, guided tours daily 9.30am–5.30pm | Piazza Verdi | 8 euros | teatromassimo.it | ⏱ 30 mins*

LA ZISA

In the 12th century, Arabian builders erected this royal summer residence for the emir. The tall cube is elegantly subdivided by decorative arches. The Moorish fountain niche, from which the water flows outside into a basin in the garden, is decorated with stalactite vaults, mosaic friezes and marble tiles. Concealed flues, clay pipes and running water create a form of air conditioning that still works 800 years after it was installed. *Tue–Sat 9am–7pm, Sun 9am–1.30pm | admission 6 euros | ⏱ 1 hr*

CONVENTO DEI CAPPUCCINI ▶

A spooky and macabre experience (not at all suitable for children!), which throws light on Sicilian piety and *memento mori* (reminder of death). Back in the day, the Capuchin friars and members of the aristocracy had themselves mummified. Covered with dust and dressed in clothes that have become cocoons, they remain preserved in the monastery catacombs. *Daily 9am–1pm and 3–5/6pm (Oct–March Sun mornings only) | admission 3 euros | ⏱ 30 mins*

PALAZZO DEI NORMANNI & CAPPELLA PALATINA ★

The former *royal palace*, the origins of which date back to the ninth century, has been the seat of the regional government of Sicily and the regional parliament since 1947. The *cappella*, the royal chapel, was embellished by Arab, Norman and Byzantine artists. The fairy-tale interior is completely covered with gold mosaics. Opposite the chancel is the richly inlaid royal throne of King Roger II (Italian: Ruggero), the Easter candlestick, the ambon used as a pulpit and the high altar. Following its restoration, the wooden Arabic "stalactite" ceiling can be seen in all its colourful magnificence. The entrance is outside the city wall. *Mon–Sat 8.30am–4.30pm, Sun 8.30am–12.30pm | Piazza Indipendenza | admission Tue–Thu 15.50 euros, Fri–Mon 19 euros | tel. for reservations 091 705 5611 | federicosecundo.org, cappellapalatina palermo.it | ⊙ 1 hr*

SAN GIOVANNI DEGLI EREMITI

In the garden of the former monastery church below the Norman palace, the sound of water gurgles and the palm trees and exotic plants flourish. Pause a while and imagine yourself in the *Arabian Nights* under the shade of Moorish domes. *Tue–Sat 9am–6pm, Sun/Mon 9am–1.30pm | admission 6 euros*

INSIDER TIP
Daydream under palms

CATTEDRALE ☂

Start by taking in the mosque-like battlements and inlaid choir before you head through the side door and into the cathedral, erected in 1185. The Norman interior was modernised and domed in the 18th century. Inside you can see the polished porphyry sarcophagi of Frederick II (1194–1250), who was called the "wonder of the world" (*stupor mundi*), and other members of the royal and imperial families. *Cathedral Mon–Sat 9am–5.30pm, Sun 9am–1pm; royal tombs Mon–Sat 9am–2pm, Sun 9am–1pm | admission 1.50 euros*

LA MARTORANA

Two churches stand on a small, palm-covered hillock. The bell tower of *La Martorana* with its delicate-looking columns and pointed arched windows became the template for many Norman churches. The interior is covered in golden mosaics by Byzantine master craftsmen. *San Cataldo* has preserved the simple structure of the stones with the Moorish red domes inside. *La Martorana Mon–Sat 9.30am–1pm and 3.30–5.30pm, Sun 9am–10.30am; San Cataldo daily 10am–6pm | admission 2 euros (La Martorana), 2.50 euros (San Cataldo)*

GALLERIA D'ARTE MODERNA (GAM)

Art from between the periods of Classicism and Art Nouveau. An

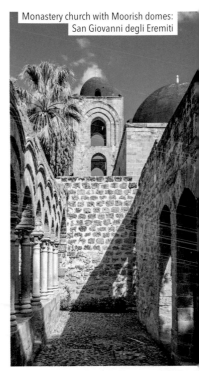

Monastery church with Moorish domes: San Giovanni degli Eremiti

excellent retrospective by Sicilian artists is displayed in the beautifully restored former monastery of *Santa Anna alla Kalsa*. *Tue–Sun 9.30am–6.30pm | Via Sant'Anna 21 | admission 8 euros | gampalermo.it |* ⏱ *1 hr*

LA KALSA

Al-Halisah, "the Chosen One", is the name the Arabs gave this district on the shore and around the harbour. It was here that the palace of the caliphs once stood. Later, the nobility built palaces and churches here, enjoyed an evening walk around the *Porta Felice* and along the sea where, today, there are lots of stalls selling fish and ice cream. However, in the past few years, La Kalsa has experienced a revival. The *Piazza Marina* with its huge 200-year-old rubber trees and masses of trattorias is lively well into the night. Lots of restoration work is going on in the main streets, *Via Alloro* and *Via Torremuzza*, which are

Sicilian delicacy from Antica Focacceria: veal spleen rolls

lined with tall Baroque palaces and churches. There is a wonderful view of the coastline and the Old Town from the *Passeggiata delle Cattive*, that runs along the city walls past the mighty Palazzo Butera.

The façade of *San Francesco d'Assisi*, with its richly decorated rose window, is impressive. The Gothic hall church is one of the few medieval churches in Palermo without any Baroque embellishments. The life-sized plasterwork allegories of virtues and vices created in 1723 by Giacomo Serpotta provide a stark contrast. A visit to *Palazzo Mirto (Tue–Sat 9am–6pm, Sun 9am–1pm | Via Merlo 2 | admission 6 euros |* ⏱ *1 hr)* provides a glimpse into the daily life of the upper class in the 18th-century. *La Magione (daily 9am–6pm | admission 4 euros)*, a plain Norman church with an enchanting cloister, borders large open areas where football-loving *ragazzi* play during the day before nightlife descends come dusk.

GALLERIA REGIONALE DELLA SICILIA 🍸

Housed in the Gothic Catalan *Palazzo Abatellis*, the museum showcases Sicily's Renaissance artistic past, including paintings on panel such as Antonello da Messina's *Annunciation*. The film-maker Wim Wenders once commented that this small picture was "more beautiful and magical than the Mona Lisa." *Tue–Sat 9am–7pm, Sun 9am–1.30pm | Via Alloro 4 | admission 8 euros |* ⏱ *1½ hrs*

ORTO BOTANICO

Take a stroll among the palms and

rubber trees. Laid out as a pleasure garden in 1792, the botanical garden today is a shady paradise with huge trees from both the Mediterranean and the Tropics. Nice café. *March/Oct daily 9am–6pm; April/Sept daily 9am–7pm; May–Aug daily 9am–8pm; Nov–Feb daily 9am–5pm | Via Lincoln 2 | admission 6 euros | ortobotanico.unipa.it | ⊙ 2 hrs*

ECOMUSEO MARE MEMORIA VIVA 🚩

Industrial architecture meets video installations. Photos and perspectives of the port capital Palermo are on display under the iron girders of this locomotive shed built in 1886. *Tue–Sat 9am–2pm | Via Messina Marinare 14 | admission free | marememoriaviva.it | ⊙ 1 hr*

WALKING WITH THE LEOPARD 🚩

You can take a tour (in English and Italian) around Palermo following

INSIDER TIP
Track Visconti's masterpiece

in the footsteps of the cult film and novel *Il Gattopardo (The Leopard)*. Garibaldi and Sciascia tours are also offered. *Sicilia Letteraria | Via Francesco Ferrara 32 | tel. 091 625 4011 | 12 euros | parcotomasi.it*

EATING & DRINKING

ANTICA FOCACCERIA SAN FRANCESCO

From nose to tail – nothing new for Palermo locals but a gourmet sensation for everyone else. If you've never tried a 🚩 spleen sandwich *(pani ca meusa)*, seasoned with organic lemon and sheep's ricotta, then you haven't tasted authentic Sicilian cuisine yet. *Daily | Via A Paternostro 58 | tel. 0 91 32 02 64 | anticafocacceria.it | €*

BISSO BISTROT

This hotspot in Quattro Canti attracts both travellers and young Palermo locals for their breakfast cornettos or to try pasta with wild fennel. *Mon–Sat | Via Maqueda 172 | mobile tel. 328 131 4595 | €€*

FUD

INSIDER TIP
Bite into a buffalo burger

Fud = food. The Big Mac is old hat: here they celebrate the triumph of the regional burger with donkey or buffalo meat. Also a branch in Catania. *Via S. Filomena 35.) Daily | Piazza Olivella 4 | tel. 091 611 2184 | fud.it | €*

POT CUCINA & BOTTEGA

Open for breakfast from 8am. Open kitchen, super, regional products and lovely cakes. *Wed–Mon | Via Garibaldi 62 | tel. 091 616 1300 | potcucina.it | €*

SHOPPING

The district between the *station, Via Roma, Piazza Cassa di Risparmio, Piazza Rivoluzione* and *Via Garibaldi* is a piece of "Old Palermo" where you can find craftspeople such as milliners, tailors, cobblers and candlemakers. At the opposite end of the scale, high-end clothes are on offer in the Art Nouveau boutiques on *Via della Libertà*.

TANTO DI COPPOLA 🚩

This is where you can buy a genuine Sicilian *coppola* from San Giuseppe Jato in any number of colours, for men, women and children, made of coarse or soft material, and for every conceivable occasion. And just to rid any doubt as to who wears this cap today: the shop is on the *Addiopizzo* list. *Via Bara all'Olivella 74 | tantodicoppola.it*

PALERMO STORE 👥

Football is king here. Dress up your *bambini* as *tifosi* from the top Sicilian football team. The pink colour on the jerseys is a nod to the city's patron saint, Rosalia. Choose a pink and black football for a souvenir. *Via Maqueda 397*

STREET MARKETS ⭐ 🚩

A feast for the eyes with plenty of background buzz. And, after a lengthy midday break, many standholders keep going well into the evening. The largest *market in the Capo district* is held around Sant'Agostino church and stretches down several roads as far as the Teatro Massimo; the 🐗 *Ballaró market* caters for the area around Porta Sant'Antonio, the Chiesa del Carmine and Chiesa del Gesù. The big *non-food market* 🐗 *Lattarini*, consisting largely of clothing and household wares, sprawls from Piazza San Domenico to Piazza Papireto. You're welcome to haggle here, which not the case when it comes to food.

NIGHTLIFE

Palermo, once known for its eerily quiet streets in the evenings because of the Mafiosi, has emerged as a party destination. Hotspots include the district around *Teatro Massimo*, the pedestrian zone of *Via Maqueda* and the *seafront promenade* with its eye-catching *Nautoscopio (Piazzetta Capitaneria del Porto)*, a crow's nest which is used as a concert stage.

BERLIN CAFÈ

This overcrowded cocktail bar serving, among other drinks, German beer, is a popular cosmopolitan haunt for Palermo's over-30 clientele. *Daily 6pm–2am | Via Isidoro La Lumia 19–21*

PUPPET THEATRE 👥 🚩

Palermo is known as the metropolis of *opera dei pupi*. Performances are held in *Mimmo Cuticchio (Via Bara all'Olivella 95 | tel. 091 323 400 | figli dartecuticchio.com)*, *Teatro Argento (Via P. Novelli 3 | tel. 091 611 3680 | palazzoasmundo.com)* and the theatre in the *Museo Internazionale delle Marionette (Piazzetta Niscemi 5 | tel. 091 328 060 | museodellemarionette. it)*. Admission from 10 euros.

AROUND PALERMO

🔲 MONTE PELLEGRINO ⭐

13km / 30 mins by car

Escape the hustle and bustle and head out into nature. Palermo's distinctive mountain is 606m high and offers

INSIDER TIP
Short but steep pilgrimage

Heaven on Earth? Gold mosaics adorn Monreale cathedral

a fantastic view over the city and the Conca d'Oro. Climb the Baroque pilgrims' path to the *pilgrimage church* dedicated to St Rosalia, the patron saint of Palermo, built into a natural cave. Palermo's residents are firm in their faith that, in times of need, their patron saint will come to their aid. *E3*

☑ MONREALE
12km / 30 mins by car

The ⭐ *Duomo di Monreale (Mon–Sat 9am–12.45pm and 2.30–4.30pm, Sun 2.30–4.45pm | admission 4 euros, combi ticket with museum, terrace and cloister 13 euros | ⏱ 2 hrs)* was founded under the Normans as a Benedictine monastery in 1174. It is the largest and most complete ecclesiastical building of that era. Inside, approached through two bronze Roman doors, the walls are covered in golden mosaics covering 6,340m². For fans of the Middle Ages, it's the eighth wonder of the world! The flora and fauna ornamentation on the 228 capitals in the cloister *(Mon–Sat 9am–1pm, Sun 9am–1.30pm | admission 6 euros)*, which has a garden and fountains,

introduces a natural element into the secluded world of the monastery. Sicilian country fare and steaks are available near the cathedral square in *Bricco & Bracco (daily | Via D'Acquisto 13 | tel. 091 641 7773 | FB | €€). E3*

☑ MONDELLO
13km / 25 mins by car

Palermo's swimming beach is not far from the city at the foot of Monte Pellegrino. Some of the Art Nouveau villas with their beautiful gardens have not yet been hemmed in by concrete blocks. The family-run *trattoria Simpaty (closed Tue and in the evenings winter | Via Piano Gallo 18 | tel. 091 454 470 | simpatymondello.com)* serves up delicious fish rolls with sultanas a little away from the hustle and bustle. *E3*

☑ BAGHERIA
18km / 40 mins by car

In the 18th and 19th centuries, the splendid villas and parks of the aristocratic families could be found close to this now concrete-covered town (pop. 53,000). The *Villa Palagonia (daily 9am–1pm, April–Oct 4–7pm, Nov–March*

3.30–5.30pm | admission 6 euros | villa-palagonia.it | (⏱ 1½ hrs), with its array of sculpted monsters and gnomes in the garden, hall of mirrors and the frescos of the Labours of Hercules inside, aroused the curiosity of illustrious travellers. The works of the Neorealist painter Renato Guttuso (1911–87), born in Bagheria, are displayed at the *Villa Cattolica (Tue–Sun 9am–5pm, April–Oct until 6pm | admission 6 euros | museoguttuso.com | (⏱ 1 hr). Trattoria Don Ciccio (closed Wed, Sun and in Aug | Via del Cavaliere 87 | tel. 091 932 442 | €)* welcomes every guest with a ⚑ hard-boiled egg and Zibibbo liqueur.

If you're looking for an experience that reaches all the senses, try the *Anchovy Museum (Mon–Sat 9.30am–12.30pm | Via Cotogni | donation 3 euros, tasting 10 euros | museodella cciuga.it | (⏱ 1½ hrs)* in the suburb of Aspra. Musician and anti-Mafia activist Michelangelo Balistreri proudly showcases colourful cans, boats and posters and arranges tasting and tours. ⊞ F3

🔟 CORLEONE
56km / 75 mins by car

This small town (pop. 10,500), famous as the home of bosses and godfathers, crops up in virtually every Mafia novel and film, which annoys many "Corleonesi". Still, there's plenty of anti-Mafia action here: In the *CIDMA (guided tours Mon–Fri 10am–5pm, Sat/Sun 10am–1pm | admission 8–15 euros, depending on number of participants | pre-booking recommended: tel. 091 8452 4295 | Via G. Valenti 7 | cidmacorleone.it)* you can look at photos and documents about the Mafia

and the struggle against the godfathers. Do your bit by buying some anti-Mafia souvenirs: olives and wine grown on land seized from Mafia clans are sold here.

INSIDER TIP
Choose anti-Mafia wine

The craggy bastion, *Rocca Busambra*, lies 1,613m above sea level in vast but barren hilly country. The mountain forests, caves and clefts in this karst landscape provided perfect hiding and burial places for the Mafia and became known as the "graveyard of the Mafia". Some of these can be reached along marked trails which start at *Bosco di Ficuzza*, the former hunting lodge of Bourbon kings. Delicious herby lamb is available at *Alpe Cucco (mobile tel. 327 761 4772 | alpecucco.it | €)*, a mountain hut reachable by car at an altitude of just under 1,000m. ⊞ E4

CEFALÙ

(⊞ G3) **The massive Norman cathedral of Cefalù (pop. 14,500) looks like a toy set against the huge rocky *Rocca* mountain.**

The roofs of the houses are clustered around the landmark of this town that was a burial place in the early Norman period and had a brief heyday as an important harbour before falling like Sleeping Beauty into a deep sleep until the 20th century. This left the medieval town virtually unaltered. The Corso Ruggero, the main street lined with austere palaces with pointed arched windows, opens onto the cathedral square. The Old Town is protected from the sea by a huge wall whose lower part is made up of centuries-old metre-high blocks. To the west of the Old Town is a large sandy beach.

SIGHTSEEING

ARABIAN WASH HOUSE
Wash your hands like they did 1,000 years ago. In the middle of the narrow Old Town is a small square that leads to a row of stone basins under low arches where several springs emerge.

MUSEO MANDRALISCA
Private collection of archaeological finds and the famous mischievous portrait of an unknown man by Antonello da Messina. *Daily 9am–7pm (in Aug until 11pm) | Via Mandralisca 13 | admission 6 euros | fondazione mandralisca.it | ⏱ 1 hr*

DUOMO DI CEFALÙ ★
The stones of this, the oldest Norman cathedral in Sicily (begun in 1140) and only completed after hundreds of years, speak volumes; the plain arches of the portico and the two massive, minaret-like façade towers are impressive. The archaic cloisters with the apse decorated with gold mosaics and the narrow transept all symbolise strength and power. *Daily 8am–12.45pm and 3.30–5.45pm | admission free, tour including cloister, tower and roof climb 8–12 euros | duomocefalu.it*

ROCCA DI CEFALÙ
La Rocca towers 268m above the town, its vertical walls protecting it from invaders. The only access is through a series of ancient walls and gateways. Flights of steps and paths lead to cisterns, ruins of buildings and a pre-Roman temple in the Cyclopean style. Remember to take water with you and wear stout shoes. *Daily 9am–7pm, Nov–March until 4pm | admission 5 euros | ⏱ 1½ hrs*

EATING & DRINKING

LE CHAT NOIR
Ignore the French name – the "Black Cat" is a genuine *osteria*. Try the house speciality: pepper salad with almonds.

Beach volleyball in Cefalù – bonus point for the old town scenery!

Fiumara d'Arte in the Tusa valley

Thu–Tue | Via XXV Novembre 17 | tel. 092 142 0697 | ristorantelechatnoir. it | €€–€€€

BEACHES

A 🏖 sandy beach begins just below the old town and stretches westwards. Beautiful beaches can be found in *Mazzaforno* (5km to the west), *Capo Caldura* (2km to the east) and *Capo Raisigerbi* (⊞ *G3*) near Finale di Pollina.

AROUND CEFALÙ

⑥ CERDA

Every year, the region celebrates an artichoke festival, "Sagra del Carciofo", and the famous vintage car race "Targa

Florio". There is an artichoke trattoria in the mountains of Cerda with a variety of vegetable antipasti. *Daily, lunch-time only | Strada Statale 120/Km 6.2 | mobile tel. 379 117 6911 | trattoria nasca2.business.site | €€. ⊞ F4*

⑦ LE MADONIE ★ ⚑
Approx. 150km round trip by car

The Madonie mountains have become a real destination for tourists in search of a bit of action. Hiking trails, cold springs and stud farms draw in many a Palermo native at weekends to stock up on salami and goat's cheese. Plus, overnight accommodation is available in mountain cabins and on farms.

The best place to start a day trip is the *pilgrimage church in Gibilmanna* which lies in a holm oak wood on the edge of the mountains. The mountain village *Isnello* is the gateway to what is Sicily's most important skiing area after Mount Etna. Mountain hikes of all degrees of difficulty can be made from spring until late autumn. *Piano Zucchi* (1,105m) and *Piano Battaglia* (1,500m), which both have cabins of the *Club Alpino Siciliano* (CAS), are the best starting points.

The intimate, child-friendly 🃏 *Agriturismo Gelso (Loc. Catalani | tel. 092 164 2310 | agriturismogelso.it | €)* is surrounded by almond groves in Castellana Sicula. It offers 🍴 cookery classes and you can nibble on almonds you've picked yourself. From Petralia, head east to *Gangi* (pop. 6,500) where the densely built houses cover the mountain like a hat. The narrow streets can only be explored on foot.

Over the *Portella di Bafurco* pass, you come up to the mountain village of *Geraci Siculo* that lies 1,077m above sea level. Tourists are still a subject of curiosity here. At the 🐟 old *village fountain* made of pink stone, locals fill up their bottles and canisters with mineral water from a nearby spring. The view from the Rocca is majestic: on a clear day, Etna, 75km away, looms like a giant above the barren mountainous countryside of central Sicily. A winding mountain road leads on through cork oak forests to Castelbuono in around 40 minutes. 🕮 *G–H4*

8 CASTELBUONO
23km / 35 mins by car

The entrance to the Old Town of Castelbuono (pop. 8,500) is guarded by the castle with the *Cappella Sant'Anna*, a masterpiece of Baroque stucco art *(daily 9.30am–5pm | admission 5 euros | museocivico.eu)*. The natural history museum, the *Museo Naturalistico Minà Palumbo (Tue–Sun 9am–1pm, 3–7pm | Piazza San Francesco | admission 3 euros | museominapalumbo.it | ⏱ 45 mins)*, is the life's work of the scientist Francesco Minà Palumbo, who walked the Madonie mountains time and again in the 19th century. The display cases contain fossils, butterflies, hand-drawn and coloured sheets of plants and stuffed birds.

Hungry? *Nangalarruni (daily | Cortile Ventimiglia 5 | tel. 092 167 1228 | hostariananangalarruni.it | €€)* serves excellent mushrooms gathered by the team. A particularly rare specimen is the white-fleshed *basiliscu*, which ripens in May. The *Fiasconaro* bar on the *piazza* has the best *panettone* south of Milan. The luxury version of the festive cake is decked with wild strawberry cream and dark Modica chocolate and comes in colourful metal boxes designed by Dolce & Gabbana. 🕮 *G4*

9 FIUMARA D'ARTE 🐖
25km / 35 mins by car

Fiumara di Tusa, the beach at *Villa Margi* and *Castel di Lucio* with its maze together form an open-air museum of modern sculpture. The ensemble has been in the making since 1986, despite major resistance from the local authorities. A real eye-catcher is the pyramid made from patinated, copper-coloured corten steel built in 2010. Colourful ceramics are made in ⚑ *Santo Stefano di Camastra* (11km east), with the shops displaying their wares beside the road. 🕮 *H3-4*

10 CAPO D'ORLANDO
80km / 70 mins by car

One thing definitely worth doing here is to enjoy an evening nightcap on the pebbly strip of ⚑ *Jack's Beach*. In summer, this small town (pop. 13,000) complete with medieval castle is flooded with families from Palermo who come to enjoy the natural beaches and diver's paradise of the adjacent Costa Saracena. The macchia vegetation of the rugged Nebrodi mountains often stretches right to the coast here. 🕮 *J3*

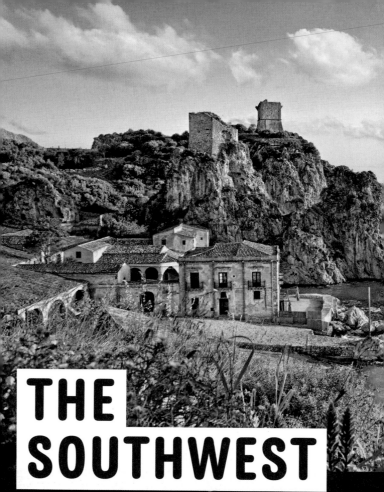

THE SOUTHWEST

SALT WORKS & ANCIENT COLUMNS

Badly bombed in 1943, Trapani has since awoken from its slumber. The restored façades, B&Bs and pubs where *ragazzi* sip bitter Guinness instead of sweet Marsala all testify to the revival of the ferry port to Tunis. The blinding and seemingly endless salt flats have become an attraction in themselves.

The Aegadian Islands, famous for tuna fishing, are generally only visited in the swimming season. North of Trapani, the Zingaro nature reserve has become a car-free hiker's paradise, while mile after

The *faraglioni* of Scopello: these cones of rock in the sea make for a great photo!

mile of vineyard stretches as far as the dessert wine stronghold of Marsala and Selinunte on the south coast.

Towards Agrigento, the few villages dotted around are perched on mountain peaks. Most visitors come for the obligatory archaeological sites: the lonely temple of Segesta, the seaside acropolis of Selinunte and the Valley of the Temples in Agrigento are often considered by connoisseurs to be more appealing than the Greek temples in the mother country.

THE SOUTHWEST

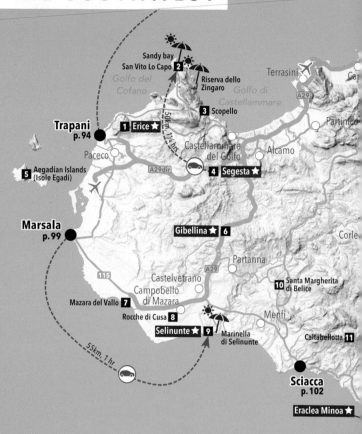

Terrasini

Golfo del Cofano

Sandy bay
San Vito Lo Capo **2**

Riserva dello Zingaro

3 Scopello

Golfo di Castellammare

Trapani p. 94

1 Erice ★

Castellammare del Golfo

Alcamo

Paceco

Partinico

A29

A29dir

4 Segesta ★

5 Aegadian Islands (Isole Egadi)

Marsala p. 99

Gibellina ★ 6

Corle

Partanna

Castelvetrano

A29

Campobello di Mazara

10 Santa Margherita di Belice

Mazara del Vallo **7**

Rocche di Cusa **8**

Menfi

Selinunte ★ 9

Marinella di Selinunte

Caltabellotta **11**

55km 1 hr

50km 1¼ hrs

Sciacca p.102

Eraclea Minoa ★

115

MARCO POLO HIGHLIGHTS

★ **ERICE**
A small, perfectly preserved medieval town ➤ p. 95

★ **SELINUNTE**
Acropolis and Hellenic temples above the sea ➤ p. 101

★ **SEGESTA**
A Greek temple and theatre in solitary mountains ➤ p. 97

★ **ERACLEA MINOA**
A magical ancient site above the snow-white chalk cliffs ➤ p. 103

★ **GIBELLINA**
A centre of modern architecture risen from the ashes of a catastrophe ➤ p. 100

★ **VALLE DEI TEMPLI**
Antiquity in its entirety: a whole valley of Greek temples ➤ p. 104

175km, 2½ hrs

Mare Tirreno

Palermo

Bagheria

A19dir

ifonte

Golfo di Termini Imerese

Cefalù

A19

Termini Imerese

A20

SICILIA

A19

Enna

Caltanissetta

Raffadali

Piazza Armerina

Siculiana Marina

13

Canicattì

Barrafranca

uliana

Agrigento p.104

Favara

Mazzarino

Riesi

Valle dei Templi ★

Porto Empedocle

Campobello di Licata **14**

Ravanusa

115

Palma di Montechiaro

15 Licata

Gela **16**

Golfo di Gela

Mare Mediterraneo

20 km
12.43 mi

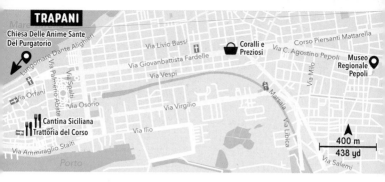

TRAPANI

(□ C3) **The town (pop. 65,000) sticks out into the sea like a long finger, with 750m-high Mount Erice towering behind. To the south is an endless flat expanse with salt pans, windmills and dazzlingly white piles of salt; the Egadi (Aegadian) Islands can be seen out at sea to the west, towards Tunis.**

The Baroque Old Town, which survived the air raids of 1943, is hidden behind the elongated harbour. The Baroque *Palazzo Riccio* has a courtyard with arcades and loggias. The *Palazzo Cavarretto* with the Sicilian eagle gracing its façade forms the end, optically, of the *Corso Vittorio Emanuele*. The magnificent ornamentation on the Jesuit church *Chiesa del Collegio* is typical of the order. The *Specus corallii* *(Via Gen. D Giglio 12)* sound cave, by Antonio Cardillo, offers cutting-edge architecture and is open for concerts.

The salt pans outside the town are still partly in operation today. Alongisde the lagoon, they are a paradise for birds. The remaining salt marsh, once with more than 60 windmills, is a listed site.

SIGHTSEEING

CHIESA DELLE ANIME SANTE DEL PURGATORIO

Popular devotion. Here in the Purgatorio church, the Passion groups for the famous

INSIDER TIP
Shockingly realistic

Good Friday night procession are on display all year round. *Via S. Francesco 33 | chiesamisteri.it*

MUSEO REGIONALE PEPOLI

You'd have to head to Asia to find craftmanship in coral carvings comparable to the works in this former convent *Santuario dell'Annunziata*. Gold work, coral carvings and majolica pieces are testimony to the skills of Trapani's master craftsmen. *Tue–Sat 9am–6pm, Sun 9am–1pm | admission 6 euros | ⊙ 1 hr*

EATING & DRINKING

CANTINA SICILIANA

Blue-tiled slow-food restaurant serving seafood with sea urchin, tuna and squid and *Cùscusu alla trapanese* (Trapanese-style couscous made with fish stock). *Via Giudecca 36 | tel. 092 328 673 | cantinasiciliana.it | €€*

TRATTORIA DEL CORSO
Signora Letizia dishes up *spaghetti alle vongole* and red mullet fillets with grapefruit. Mouthwatering. *Closed Sun lunchtime (except in summer) | Corso Italia 51 | tel. 092 323 475 | €–€€*

SHOPPING

CORALLI E PREZIOSI 🏳
Giusi Damiano and Alfonso Graffeo, two young gold-smiths, bring new life to Trapani's coral tradition. You can watch them create their internationally acclaimed items of jewellery in their workshop. *Via A. Roasi 11 | corallipreziosi.it*

INSIDER TIP
Coral-red jewellery

AROUND TRAPANI

🔟 ERICE ⭐
8km/30mins by car, then by bus to the valley station and a 10-min cable-car ride

Virtually directly above the sea at a height of 700m, is the medieval town of Erice with its grey stone houses. It is often hidden in the clouds, even when the sun is blazing down on the rest of western Sicily. The view over the plains and salt pans, the islands in the shallow sea off Marsala, the Isole Egadi (Aegadian Islands) and the rocky

Salt is still harvested from the Trapani salt pans

coastline of San Vito is quite exceptional. The Elymians and Phoenicians from Asia Minor worshipped Astarte, the goddess of love, and the Romans built a large sanctuary to Venus on the site of the present-day *Norman castle*. Many Sicilians visit at the weekend to enjoy the cooler air. The quickest way to reach this mountain eyrie is by cable car *(mid-April–early Jan, core times Mon 2–8pm, Tue–Fri 9am–8pm, Sat/Sun 9.30am–8.30pm, depending on the season also earlier in the morning, in summer later in the evening | single ticket, return 9.50 euros | funiviaerice.it)*.

Try Sicilian top wines at *Monte San Giuliano (closed Mon | tel. 092 386 9595 | montesangiuliano.it | €€)* which also serves the famous *cuscus alla trapanese*. ▥ C3

🞭 SAN VITO LO CAPO

38km/55 mins by car

The 40km journey along the jagged coastline is magnificent. Bare rock in *Scurati* with inhabited farmhouses next to deserted houses built in a huge cave. Further inland, the *macchia* becomes denser, broken up by small fields. This is the start of a trail around the 659m-high *Monte Cofano*, a nature reserve that cannot be missed. The circular tour takes approx. three to four hours, including a break along the craggy coastline to go for a swim with wonderful views of the shore, the islands and the Zingaro mountain range.

San Vito (pop. 4,800) lies in a shallow 🏖 sandy bay close to the promontory with the lighthouse. It has grown up around a mighty Saracen tower that has since been converted into a church. The exposed site, the sandy beach and the bizarre cliff formations of *Torre dell'Impiso* have made this into a popular tourist resort. San Vito is well known for its 🏴 couscous with fish and seafood and a couscous festival is held every year in September, with people making the journey from as far away as Angola. In the other 50 weeks of the year, you can find this speciality at *Alfredo (Tue–Sun | Contrada Valanga 3 | tel. 092 397 2366 | €€)*, on the outskirts of the town, where the spaghetti with fresh prawns can also be recommended. You could also try *Pocho (evenings only | tel. 092 397 2525 | pocho.it | €€)* in Makari, 5km to the south, where the philosopher Marilù Terrasi runs the small hotel offering interesting cuisine and organises musical and theatrical events. ▥ C3

INSIDER TIP
Cook-off: Africa vs Europe

🞭 SCOPELLO

35km/50 mins by car

Scopello is little more than a fortified farming hamlet located above the cliffs and surrounded by a wall with barren *macchia* beyond. The sea thrashes onto tiny pebbly bays below that are dominated by the *faraglioni* – the high, rugged cliffs. To the north is the boundary of *Zingaro* nature reserve. The old shepherds' cottages are now lived in by local craftsmen or are small country guesthouses.

A road leads to the *Riserva dello Zingaro (▥ C–D3)*, although the actual nature reserve can only be accessed on foot. Don't forget your swimming things as there are any number of little paths down to romantic  bays. Fan palms grow in this area in the thousands, and can reach a height of 4–5m. You are not allowed to leave the well-tended paths; dogs are not permitted.

A 7km-long path along the coast is signposted and easy walking, but remember to take lots of water, something to eat and sunscreen. *(Information at both entrances, in Scopello and Torre dell'Uzzo | daily 7am–7.30pm | admission incl. hiking map 5 euros | riservazingaro.it).* Allow approx. four hours for the coastal path, there and back; for the circular path halfway up and then back along the coast allow five or six hours.

Ristorante del Golfo (closed Mon/ Tue lunchtime | Via Segesta 153 | tel. 092 430 257 | ristorantedelgolfo.it | €€), in the centre of Castellammare, serves sea urchin spaghetti and scabbard fish with pistachios and is just 10km southeast along the coast. *D3*

4 SEGESTA ★
33km/30 mins by car

In a solitary location in the mountains are the remains of the amphitheatre and temple of an Elymian town, whose residents had adopted the Greek culture and lifestyle, that has long since disappeared. The fifth-century *temple* was probably never actually completed. The *amphitheatre* further up opens up to the distant sea and the valley below Alcamo. *Daily 9am–7.30pm; March–Oct until 6pm;*

Nov–Feb until 5pm | admission 6 euros | ⏱ 2 hrs

On the *Fiume Caldo* below Segesta there are thermal springs with a high sulphur content that surface at the end of a deep gorge. Along the Castellammare road take the turning to 🌡 *Terme Segestane (thermally heated swimming pool Fri–Wed 10am–1pm and 4.30–11pm, closed Mon mornings | admission 10 euros | termesegestane.com)* after the bridge

German writer Goethe was impressed by the well-preserved temple of Segesta

Azzurro! You'll need a boat to reach many of Favignana's beautiful bays

over the river. Free spa facilities are available at 🐟 *Polle di Crimiso (Bagni liberi di Segesta)* in Ponte Bagni. 🕮 *D4*

5 AEGADIAN ISLANDS (ISOLE EGADI)

19/15/41km / 40/30/80 mins by hydrofoil

Ferries and hydrofoils cross to the three islands off Trapani. The small limestone islands are surrounded by unpolluted waters; the caves and rich underwater life are a particular draw for divers.

Favignana (19km², 33km coastline, pop. 4,300) is still one of the most important tuna fisheries today. Soft volcanic tuff was once quarried along the mostly flat rocky coastline for use in the building trade. The bizarre shapes of these quarries right on the shore can still be seen. Most of the island is flat and covered with fields, but in the middle is the 314m-high *Monte Santa Caterina* with a fortress on the top. Bays suitable for swimming and a few sandy patches can be found in the south of the island. For the best seafood try *Egadi (Via Colombo 17 | tel. 092 392 1232 | albergoegadi.it | €€–€€€)*.

Levanzo (6km², 12km coastline, pop. 150) is a 278m-high rocky outcrop which, apart from the fields on the flat part of the island and the terraces above the harbour, is covered by thick *macchia*. The coastline is rugged and rocky. The *Grotta del Genovese (tours from the harbour daily 9am–1.30pm | ⏱ 2 hrs | 30 euros incl. admission | bookings tel. 092 392 4032 | mobile tel. 339 741 8800 | grottadelgenovese.it)* is a prehistoric cult site. The drawings of animals carved into the rock are approx. 12,000 years old, while the wall paintings are some 5,000 years old. If you're feeling brave, try fresh sea urchins *(ricci di mare)* at *Paradiso (daily | Via Lungomare 8 | tel. 092 392 4080 | FB: AlbergoRistorante ParadisoLevanzo | €€).*

Marettimo (12km², 19km coastline, pop. 700) has a cragged mountain ridge rising 686m out of the sea. There are only a few places where the sea can be accessed easily, and the marvellous bays and caves are best reached by boat *(tours from the harbour)*. Underwater, Marettimo is a dreamworld. Hikers can follow goat paths up the eastern flank of the island to the ruined fortress *Punta Troia* and to the lighthouse on the west coast The *trattoria Il Pirata (daily | tel. 092 392 302/ | €€)* is the island's meeting place; their specialty is pasta with lobster. ⌕ *A–B 3–4*

MARSALA

(⌕ B4) **Capo Lilibeo, the most westerly point of Sicily, is part of the town of Marsala (pop. 82,000) and is the place where Garibaldi landed in 1860 and set about conquering the island. Marsala is world famous as the wine centre of western Sicily.**

John Woodhouse is to be thanked for this status. While under Napoleonic rule, he created Marsala fortified wine as a substitute for the much-loved port so missed by the English. You can try and buy it in many wine cellars in the town. Marsalas are increasingly dry.

SIGHTSEEING

OLD TOWN

The pretty Baroque town lies inside the largely intact town walls. The *Piazza della Repubblica* hosts tango dancing in front of the cathedral of *San Tommaso* on summer nights. *Vuoi ballare?* Come and join in!

MUSEO ARCHEOLOGICO BAGLIO ANSELMI

The remains of a Punic ship from the third century BCE that was raised in 1969 off Marsala can be seen here. The museum also includes finds from the Punic and Roman settlement. *Sun 9am–1pm, Tue–Sat 9am–6pm | on Capo Lilibeo | admission 4 euros | ⏱ 1 hr*

CANTINA MARCO DE BARTOLI ☂

The former racing driver Marco de Bartoli is seen as the pioneer of the new dry Marsala wine and pure wine made from autochthonous, traditional grape varieties. You can taste his oenological heritage on an enjoyable 60- to 90-minute guided tour. *Mon–Fri, approx. 10am and 3pm | Contrada Samperi | booking tel. 092 396 2093 | 20–200 euros | marcodebartoli.com*

INSIDER TIP
Marsala doesn't have to be sweet

EATING & DRINKING

IL GALLO E L'INNAMORATA

Fish rice arancini or tuna in mint sauce are served in this *osteria* in the old town. *Closed Mon | Via Stefano Bilardello 18 | tel. 092 3195 4446 | osteriailgalloelinnamorata.it | €€*

AROUND MARSALA

6 GIBELLINA ★
57km/70 mins by car

Following the earthquake in 1968, temporary shelters were built in Belice Valley that threatened to become a permanent feature. Funding was diverted into the pockets of the Mafia and corrupt politicians. Gibellina had been devastated and the residents fought the resulting exodus and invited artists who drew attention to Gibellina and the reconstruction efforts. The old village is a sea of debris, partly overgrown and partly a concrete monument. Alberto Burri's *Cretto* is continuously growing and is thought to be the largest work of land art in Europe with regard to the area it covers. The new settlement is 20km away. It is an urban experiment with remarkable modern architectural designs and a pleasant and spaciously laid-out residential landscape with gardens, which is, in part, already deteriorating again.

In the *Museo delle Trame Mediterranee (Tue–Sun 9am–1pm, 3–6pm | admission 6 euros | fondazioneorestiadi.it |* ◷ *1 hr)* in Baglio di Stefano just outside the town, works by classical modernist and contemporary artists (Joseph Beuys, Giorgio de Chirico, Renato Guttuso) are on display. Couscous and pizza are served at *Ristorante Massara (closed Tue | Via Vespri Siciliani 29 | tel. 092 467 871 | €–€€)*.

The large spa 🛁 *Terme di Acqua Pia (in summer daily 9am–midnight | admission 13–15 euros | tel. 092 539 026 | termeacquapia.it)* and its natural pool "Cascatelle" and swimming pools is situated on the road to Montevago (20km southeast) with a pool, spa area, hot springs, park and restaurant *(€)*. ⅏ D4

7 MAZARA DEL VALLO
23km/35 mins by car

Sicily's largest fishing port employs many Tunisian workers. The Old Town is rather like a *kasbah* – white and plain, with just a few solitary palm trees towering over it. The *Piazza della Repubblica* is a beacon in the Baroque design of squares while the interior of the *cathedral* is an example of the exceptional quality of Sicilian stucco craftsmanship and the ability to imitate every conceivable material using plaster, gold leaf and paint. Maritime archaeological finds are displayed in the *Museo del Satiro (daily 9am–7pm | Piazza Plebiscito | admission 6 euros |* ◷ *30 mins)* in the former church of Sant'Egidio. The highlight is the dancing Satyr, a 2m-high bronze statue from the fourth century BCE.

Mussel lovers head for the *Trattoria delle Cozze Basiricò (on the coast road to Torre Granitola | tel. 092 394 2323 | trattoriadellecozze.it | €)*. And if you're hoping to soak up some of the local beauty, book a Sicilian treatment with sea salt, lemons and olive oil at the 🛁 spa of the *Almar Giardino di Costanza (Via Salemi Km 7 | tel. 036 544 1139 | almargiardinodicostanza.com)*. ⅏ C5

8 ROCCHE DI CUSA 🐷

47km/55 mins by car

Column drums and capitals intended for the construction of the gigantic temple in Selinunte, which were never used, have been lying in the ancient quarry Rocche di Cusa on the edge of Campobello di Mazara for 2,500 years. The 1km-long and narrow archaeological area is a picturesque natural site with almond trees. *Admission 2 euros | same opening times as Selinunte |* 📖 *C5*

9 SELINUNTE ⭐

55km / 60 mins by car

The Greek temples on an elevated plateau above the sea can be seen from a long way away. More impressive than the rebuilt columns are the huge piles of stones that are the ruins of Temple G, tempting visitors to climb. The largest part of this ancient city still lies hidden

in the earth. The distances within the excavation zone alone and the size of the *Acropolis (daily 9am–7pm, ticket office closes at 6pm | admission 6 euros | ⏱ 2½ hrs)* give some idea as to the dimensions of this ancient city, whose heyday resulted from the wheat trade and lasted just 300 years.

The modern coastal resort of *Marinella di Selinunte* has extensive sandy beaches, especially around the mouth of the River Belice. The restaurant *Africa (closed Thu | Via Alceste 24 | mobile tel. 388 371 2814 | €€)* on the promenade is praised for its wide range of pizzas. 📖 *D5*

10 SANTA MARGHERITA DI BELICE

70km/75 mins by car

Have you heard of Luchino Visconti's cinema classic *The Leopard*? The family of the author Giuseppe Tomasi di

Gibellina under cement: the monumental "Cretto" by Alberto Burri

Lampedusa owned the large palace *Filangeri Cutò* in Santa Margherita di Belice which, after being destroyed by an earthquake in 1968, was rebuilt on the same site. It is now home to the literature museum *Museo del Gattopardo (Thu–Tue 9am–1pm, 3–6.30pm, Sun morning only | admission 5 euros, guided tour 7 euros | ۞ 1 hr)*, containing salons, various various wax figures, scripts, film screenings, a recording with the voice of the author and photographs. ⊞ D5

SCIACCA

(⊞ D5) **The avalanche of buildings of Sciacca (pop. 39,000) that tumbles down the hill to the fishing harbour looks like an oriental kasbah.**

The Old Town is a labyrinth only accessible on foot; many streets are just wide enough for two people to pass. The steps to the upper parts of the town date largely from the Arab period.

The Old Town is surrounded by a wall with lovely Baroque gates. The main thoroughfare, the *Corso Vittorio Emanuele*, is lined by palatial residences and the churches. Locals meet for their evening ▶ *corso* on the large square in front of the Jesuit college. After passing the delightful Baroque *cathedral* you reach the well-kept *municipal park* and the (closed) *thermal baths*, very much in the turn-of-the-20th-century style when the hot springs and steam fumaroles

of Sciacca made it one of the major spa resorts in Europe.

In the 20th-century, Filippo Bentivegna created a bizarre, Baroque-like collection of sculptures with exaggerated features. Row upon row of sculpted stone heads can now be seen in his olive grove. He bequeathed his *Castello Incantato (daily 9am–1pm and 4–8pm, July/Aug 9am–8pm, in winter 9am–1pm and 3–5pm | admission 5 euros | ۞ 45 mins)* to the town of Sciacca.

EATING & DRINKING

HOSTARIA DEL VICOLO
In the upper part of the Old Town, this restaurant serves spaghetti with mint and tuna fish roe, as well as Baroque-style monastery desserts. *Closed Mon | Vicolo Sammaritano 10 | tel. 092 523 071 | hostariadelvicolo.it | €€€*

OSTERIA IL GRAPPOLO
Salvatore Ciaccio prepares delicacies such as broad bean purée or breaded scabbardfish. Products from the family-owned farm complete the menu. *Closed Tue | Via Conzo 9A | tel. 092 585 294 | FB: OsteriailGrappoloSciacca | €–€€*

BEACHES

Sandy bays can be found along the road to Agrigento: *Torre Macauda, Torre Verdura* and *Secca Grande* as well as the large nature reserve at the mouth of the *Fiume Platani* that stretches as far as *Capo Bianco* below Eraclea Minoa. Secca Grande is a must for divers.

Fish is sold fresh off the boat in the port of Sciacca – just like the rest of Sicily

AROUND SCIACCA

🆕 CALTABELLOTTA

20km/35 mins by car

Many places in Sicily have been built in daring locations but few are like Caltabellotta, below a range of cliffs with castles and churches growing out of the rock. 🏴 Authentic recipes such as wild asparagus *frittata*, suckling pig with mint or sweet *cannoli* are served in the authentic and rustic trattoria M.A.T.E.S. (closed Sun evenings | Vicolo Storto 3 | tel. 092 595 2327 | matesonline.it | €–€€), reminding guests of the traditional Jewish olive oil trade. 🗺 E5

🆕 ERACLEA MINOA ★

33km/35 mins by car

The snow-white chalk cliffs southeast of Sciacca drop 80m vertically into the sea. Above, on the flat, are the remains of the ancient town. The *amphitheatre (daily 9.30am–7.30pm, in winter until 4.30/5.30pm | admission 4 euros | ⏱ 45 mins)*, carved out of the soft stone, is now protected from further erosion under a plexiglass roof.

In nearby Montallegro, *Relais Briuccia (Via Trieste 1)* is housed in a restored former nobleman's palace. At the associated restaurant, *Capitolo Primo (closed Mon | mobile tel. 339 759 21 76 | ristorantecapitoloprimo.it | €€–€€€)*, Damiano Ferraro shows what he has learned at top European restaurants. 🗺 E6

AGRIGENTO

(□ F6) **Stop in the provincial capital of Agrigento: you'll want to see the honey-yellow Greek temples hidden among almond and olive groves.**

The romantic antiquity at the foot of the medieval Girgenti, not too far from the skyscrapers of modern Agrigento (pop. 56,000), captivated tourists even when people were still drawing rather than snapping photos for social media.

SIGHTSEEING

VALLE DEI TEMPLI ★

"The citizens of Akragas build as if they would live forever, and eat as if they would die tomorrow," once said a Greek poet. If you want to admire this frenzy of building today, you need to take a walk down the temple road. Start at the entrance at the *Temple of Juno/Hera (Tempio di Giunone o Hera)*, the highest point, where it is less crowded and easier to park. Although marauding Carthaginians had set the sea-view sanctuary on fire by 406 BCE, most of the columns are still standing, as are some gnarled olive trees that could have thousands of years under their belts. Below you can see the funereal *Tomb of Theron*. Along the steep slope, a walkway leads to the *Temple of Concorde*. This classical Doric temple from the fifth century BCE owes its exceptional condition to its conversion into a Christian church. Above an always-crowded car park, you can see the piles of stones of the

Temple of Heracles of which eight columns are still standing.

Cross the car park and enter the archaeological zone. The *Temple of Olympian Zeus* is a pile of huge blocks of stone and column drums. Building work on the colossal structure started following the victory over the Carthaginians at Himera in 480 BCE. With a length of 112m and a width of 58m, it was one of the largest temples in the ancient world. The Carthaginians destroyed the incomplete building in 406 BCE. At the far boundary of the lower level with remains of a holy site is the *Sanctuary of the Chthonic Gods (Tempio delle divinità ctonie)* with sacrificial pits and the *Temple of Castor and Pollux. Daily 8.30am–8pm | admission 10 euros, with museum ticket 13.50 euros |* ⏱ *3 hrs.*

From around July to mid-September, the temples are illuminated at night INSIDER TIP **Big temple show** *(Mon–Fri until 11pm, Sat/Sun until midnight, ticket office closes 1 hr earlier)*. Sunset tours in English usually start at 6.15, 6.45 and 8pm *(to book: lavalledeitempli.it | 20 euros, minimum 9 people or 130 euros plus entrance fee)*.

After so much hardcore archaeology, why not relax in the adjacent *Giardino della Kolymbetra (daily 10am–5/6pm, July/Aug until 9.30pm; winter 10am–2pm | admission 7 euros)*, a natural paradise with orange groves, almond and olive trees. There are also subterranean springs whose water was used to irrigate the valley and for fish farming. It all calls for a picnic!

MUSEO ARCHEOLOGICO REGIONALE 🌴

Greek vases and a model of the 7.75m-high telamon from the Temple of Zeus, thought to support the roof, can be seen in one of the rooms. The Romanesque monastery church of *San Nicola*, where you can see the Phaedra sarcophagus from Late Antiquity depicting the tragic love of Phaedra and her stepson Hippolytus, also belongs to the museum. *Tue–Sat 9am–7pm | admission 8 euros, incl. excavations 13.50 euros | ⏱ 1½ hrs.*

OLD TOWN

Often forgotten, the home town of Nobel literature laureate Luigi Pirandello (1867–1936) is a maze of stairs with an urban buzz during the evening *corso* on *Via Atenea*. The centre is the *Piazzale Aldo Moro* with its many palm trees that links the medie-

The surviving columns of the Temple of Heracles tower are over 10 m high

val part with the modern town. The Cistercian abbey of *Santo Spirito* is a hidden gem. The B&B is

famous for its marzipan lambs at Easter *(short.travel/siz5)*.

The *Cattedrale di San Gerlando* (in danger of collapsing) is on the highest point of the Old Town. Its large interior with octagonal pillars and richly carved coffered ceiling is impressive.

EATING & DRINKING

KOKALOS

Travel groups are attracted to this restaurant's pretty garden with views of the temple. Pizzas from the wood-fired oven in the evenings. *Daily | Via Alfredo Capitano 3 | tel. 092 260 6427 | ristorante-kokalos.net | €*

ROSTICCERIA PALUMBO 🍴

Simple but delicious. Choose from roast chicken with rosemary, rice arancini or antipasti to take away. *Thu–Tue, Sun at lunchtime only | Piazza Pirandello 26 | tel. 092 229 765 | €*

DA CARMELO

Somewhere for those who love something a bit different. Snails, rabbit, lamb and kid, to name a few, are served in this village trattoria in

Scala dei Turchi: the white "Turkish staircase" rises from the sea near Agrigento

Joppolo Giancaxio, 12km north. *Thu–Tue evenings only, Sun also lunch | Via Roma 16 | Joppolo Giancaxio | 12km north | tel. 092 263 1376 | €*

SPORT & ACTIVITIES

AKRAGAS EXPRESS
Ideal for groups and special occasions: this nostalgic railway trip will whisk you from Agrigento to Porto Empedocle with a stopover at the remote Temple of Hephaestus and the chance to visit the Kolymbethra Garden. *Mobile tel. 329 957 0774 | ferroviekaos.it*

AROUND AGRIGENTO

🔟 SICULIANA
26km/35 mins by car
Between Porto Empedocle and Sciacca the main road runs 3–8km inland

from the coast with smaller roads leading off to secluded beaches. Near Realmonte (20km from Agrigento), snow-white sandstone cliffs at *Capo Rosello* drop 90m into the sea below. For a similarly spectacular and just as snow-white walk above the coast, head for *Scala dei Turchi*. In Realmonte, fans of dry-aged steaks will get more than their money's worth at the *Osteria dei Folli (closed Wed in winter | Piazza Umberto I 27 | tel. 092 281 4185 | €€)*. Plus, they serve organic vegetables from their own garden.

Apart from a rocky coastline, *Siculiana Marina* has a flat sandy beach that stretches as far as Torre Salsa. *La Scogliera (closed Mon | tel. 092 281 7532 | €€)* on the promenade along the shore serves good seafood. The dunes at *Torre Salsa* line the 6km-long beach and form part of the World Wildlife Fund nature reserve that covers some 761 hectares *(entrance at the visitor centre | tel. 092 281 8220 | wwftorresalsa.it)*. 🔲 E6

14 CAMPOBELLO DI LICATA
50km/50 mins by car

Since 1980, the Argentinian artist Silvio Benedetto has been designing squares, decorating façades with murals, sculpting and creating wall and floor mosaics in this former mining town (pop. 9,500). *From Inferno to Paradise*: in the 🐂 *Valle delle Pietre Dipinte (summer Tue–Sun 9am–1pm, 4–8pm | suggested donation | mobile tel. 334 905 7909)*, characters and scenes from Dante's *Divine Comedy* have been depicted on 110 travertine slabs. If you prefer something more classical, scenes and figures from Homer's *Iliad* on 24 ceramic tiles create one large image (7×3m) in the auditorium. *silviobenedetto.com* | 💷 *G6*

15 LICATA
44km/45 mins by car

This harbour town (pop. 35,000) is a fabulous place to eat: Pino Cuttaia, twice Michelin starred,

INSIDER TIP
Fine dining from a star Sicilian chef

offers one of the most creative cuisines in Sicily, including scabbardfish or Nebrodi pork grilled on almond shells, at La Madia *(closed Tue, Sun evenings in winter | Via Filippo Re Capriata 22 | tel. 092 277 1443 | ristorantelamadia.it | €€€)*. If you're looking for something less expensive, try the *"poesia di terra e di mare"* by Peppe Bonsignore at *L'Oste e il Sacrestano (closed Sun evening and Mon | Via S Andrea 19 | tel. 092 277 4636 | losteeilsacrestano.it | €€)*. 💷 *G7*

En route to Licata, you pass through *Palma di Montechiaro (💷 F6)* and the ancestral home of the family of the novelist Giuseppe Tomasi di Lampedusa. *Marina di Palma* is just 4km away where the cliffs are dominated by a ruined castle.

16 GELA
75km/75 mins by car

This industrial town (pop. 74,000) and former Mafia stronghold is worth a detour to see the Greek town walls at *Capo Soprano*. The *Museo Regionale Archeologico (Mon–Sat 9am–7pm | admission 4 euros | ⏱ 1 hr)*, next to the Parco Rimembranza, boasts a number of valuable finds and a remarkable coin collection. The trattoria 🚩 *San Giovanni (closed Sun | Via Damaggio Fischetti 51 | tel. 093 391 2674 | €)* offers a young regional cuisine and a delicious *caponata*. The beach in *Falconara*, 20km towards Agrigento, with a castle in the background, is lovely. 💷 *H7*

WHERE TO SLEEP IN AGRIGENTO

AT HOME WITH THE ARISTOCRACY
Romantic five-star luxury with spa, fine-dining restaurant and temple views in a baronial palace in Agrigento at Villa Athena *(27 rooms | Via Passeggiata Archeologica 33 | tel. 092 259 6288 | hotelvilla athena.it | €€€)*.

THE AEOLIAN ISLANDS

CAPER FLOWERS & VOLCANIC BEACHES

Whitewashed cubic farmhouses with loggias overgrown with plumbago and bougainvillea – independent tourism is writ large on the *Isole Eolie*, named for the god of wind, Aeolos. After all, the islands are home to a colourful array of people – sun worshippers, yacht owners, mountaineers and proud non-drivers. What links them is a love of nature and real Mediterranean cuisine. Since 1999, the archipelago has also been a UNESCO World Natural and Cultural Heritage Site.

A serpentine road snakes its way to the lighthouse of Gelso on Vulcano

From afar, the Aeolian (or Lipari) islands of Vulcano, Salina, Panarea, Stromboli, Filicudi and Alicudi look like silvery-grey cones hovering above the water. As you draw closer, their volcanic origin as part of the underwater volcano of Marsili becomes perfectly obvious. Crashing waves have gnawed at the soft tuff and blocks of harder lava can be found along the shoreline which drops steeply into the sea. Caves, grottoes and arches, small rocky islets and tiny coves and beaches make up an unspoilt coastline.

THE AEOLIAN ISLANDS

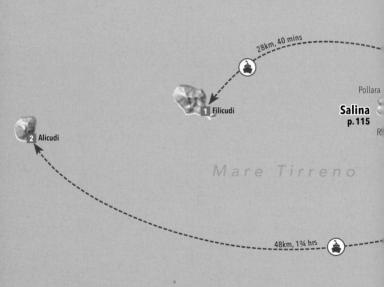

M a r e

M e d i t e r r a n e o

28km, 40 mins

1 Filicudi

Pollara

Salina
p. 115

R

2 Alicudi

M a r e   T i r r e n o

48km, 1¾ hrs

MARCO POLO HIGHLIGHTS

★ **ACROPOLIS/NATIONAL MUSEUM**
Archaeology meets vulcanology in Lipari
➤ p. 113

★ **STROMBOLI**
Naturally spectacular: the island's
924m-high active volcano ➤ p. 116

★ **PUNTA MILAZZESE**
A prehistoric village on the southern cape
of Panarea ➤ p. 118

★ **VULCANO**
A smoking crater and sulphurous hot
springs ➤ p. 119

10 km
6.22 mi

Capo d'Orlando

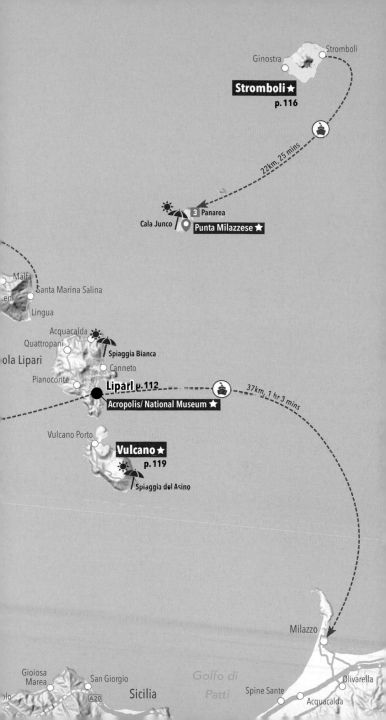

Ginostra

Stromboli

Stromboli ★

p. 116

22km, 25 mins

☀ 3 Panarea

Cala Junco

Punta Milazzese ★

Malfa

Santa Marina Salina

en

Lingua

Acquacalda

☀

Quattropani

Spiaggia Bianca

ola Lipari

Canneto

Pianoconte

Lipari p. 112

37km, 1 hr 3 mins

Acropolis/ National Museum ★

Vulcano Porto

Vulcano ★

p. 119

☀

Spiaggia del Asino

Milazzo

Gioiosa
Marea

San Giorgio

*Golfo di
Patti*

Olivarella

A20

Sicilia

Spine Sante

Acquacalda

olo

A moment of peace: Lipari's main street and promenade is Via Vittorio Emanuele

The Aeolian Islands were first settled by seafarers 6,000 years ago, who traded in obsidian; the shiny, black, volcanic glass used to make sharp blades and arrowheads was exported as far as Scandinavia. Today, the igneous rock is used in costume jewellery.

"La cucina eoliana", the islanders' cuisine, was the result of an extremely poor people scraping a living from farming and fishing who wanted to gain some pleasure from their food. Even today, the food they cook makes careful use of what the sea and the land provide. The sun, the salty sea air and the minerals in the volcanic earth give an especially intensive aroma to the tomatoes, aubergines, courgettes and greens. This is accentuated by wild fennel, oregano and capers that no dish goes without and which grow in abundance on the islands.

A useful piece of information is that ferries and hydrofoils *(aliscafi)* operate between Milazzo *(&plnstar; L3)* and Lipari (the central point for reaching all the other islands) several times a day. The *traghetto* also takes cars!

LIPARI

(&plnstar; K2) **This is the Italy you know from picture books. The harbour bars and boutiques of Lipari (pop. 4,500) are the perfect place to relax. With its Baroque façades and capped church towers, the town is dwarfed by the massive rock of the Acropolis (citadel) and its fortress that was built in the Middle Ages.**

The houses nestle around the two bays, the *Marina Lunga* where the ferries come in, and the lively *Marina Corta*. In front of the Marina Corta is the little chapel island and there are bars and restaurants around the *piazza*. The small 🔭 *Chiesa delle Anime del Purgatorio* is home to a permanent and charming sea nativity scene. Can you be the first to spot the potbellied fisherman, the donkey and the holy couple?

Behind the marina, the narrow streets quickly get wider as they lead up to the Acropolis and into the old town. These are followed by the new straight network of roads with houses and gardens, the majority of the hotels and the main thoroughfare, the *Via Vittorio Emanuele*. It's hard to believe that this charming island once served as a place of exile during the fascist era. The town is surrounded by hills with terraced fields created at considerable effort, which – both here and on the other side of the island – are gradually being abandoned.

SIGHTSEEING

ACROPOLIS/NATIONAL MUSEUM ★

The appearance of the citadel – the upper town with churches and noblemen's houses – dates from the Baroque period. Located above the rugged cliffs, this knoll had previously been used for centuries by the locals as a place of refuge from pirate raids. Reconstructed early tombs and traces of settlements can be seen opposite the cathedral of *San Bartolomeo* with its Norman cloister.

In Antiquity and early history, the Aeolian Islands were a central point for trading throughout the Mediterranean. Rich finds from this time are exhibited in the palaces on the Acropolis. One of the highlights is a unique collection of Hellenic theatrical masks made of terracotta, as well as amphorae recovered by underwater archaeologists. There is also a section on volcanology. *Mon–Sat 9am–7.30pm, Sun 9am–1.30pm | admission 10 euros |* ⏱ *1 hr.*

EATING & DRINKING

GILBERTO E VERA

Traditional island establishment at the Marina Corta serving the freshest panini and offering an enormous selection of wine from all over Italy. To bite into a freshly topped *panino vulcano*, with capers, Calabrian salami and pepperoncino oil is to taste Lipari. *Daily in the summer | Via Garibaldi 22 | tel. 090 981 2756 | €*

KASBAH ▶

This casual meeting point with olive garden offers a reinterpretation of island cooking. Lamb with tomato foam or kamut pasta with artichokes. Plus possibly Lipari's best pizza and popcorn gelato. *Daily in summer | Vico Selinunte 43 | tel. 090 981 1075 | FB: kasbah.lipari | €–€€€*

OSTERIA LIPAROTA

In an alley near the small harbour, young chef Franco Matarazzo serves roasted *pulpo* with chickpea purée, to

Bright, refreshing and delicious: the *granita* at Da Alfredo on Salina

name just one delicacy. *Daily | Corso Vittorio Emanuele II 34 | mobile tel. 333 221 082 | €€*

SHOPPING

Via Vittorio Emanuele is the place to go for pretty clothing, obsidian jewellery and, of course, capers.

GIOVANNI SPADA

Unique Mediterranean souvenirs. Do you prefer Aphrodite or Hermes? Terracotta replicas of Greek gods and theatre masks, ranging from representations

INSIDER TIP
Buy your very own god!

of the promiscuous hetaerae to the miser, are sold here. *Via Vittorio Emanuele 199*

SPORT & ACTIVITIES

Boats to the neighbouring islands, beaches and bays depart from the Marina Corta. *Da Massimo (Via Maurolico 2 | tel. 090 981 3086 | damassimo.it)* has rubber boats for hire. Scooters and boats can be rented from *Roberto Foti (Via F Crispi 30 | tel. 090 981 1370 | robertofoti.it). Amici delle Eolie (Via Garibaldi 37 | mobile tel. 338 158 4128 | amicidelleeolie.it)* offers fishing trips. Snorkellers should contact the diving school *La Gorgonia (Salita San Giuseppe | tel. 090 981 2616 | lagorgoniadiving.it)*

NIGHTLIFE

MARINA CORTA ☂

The area next to the former Aliscafi terminal is basically a huge open-air bar where the fishermen dock. If you're lucky, a local will play a guitar solo for you of an evening.

AROUND LIPARI

TOUR OF THE ISLAND

33km / approx. 90 mins by taxi/ minibus

A *giro dell'isola* is a must: the island can be explored by taking the circular tour with the local father-son taxi company *Mirko e Bartolo (mobile tel. 368 675 400 and 338 196 6378).* Both men are extremely proud to show visitors the most beautiful panoramas and the former pumice quarries. During the tour, make sure to stop at *Canneto's* rubble beach and look for obsidian splinters at *Forgia Vecchia*. A footpath in front of a now-disused pumice quarry leads to 🏃 *Spiaggia Bianca*, Lipari's most popular beach.

Beyond *Acquacalda*, the road climbs up to the plateau and the farming communities of *Quattropani* and *Pianoconte*. The *Terme di San Calogero* spa has been abandoned for years, but if you're lucky, the elderly curator Mimmo will show you a Mycenaean steam bath for a tip.

From the *belvedere* you have a wonderful view of the neighbouring island, Vulcano – a vista sought by many a camera. You can also taste the fruit from the mulberry trees at the small car park. *K2*

SALINA

(J2) **Salina, with its extinct double volcanoes, Monte Fossa delle Felci (962m) and Monte dei Porri (860m), is also known as the "green island" due to is its extensive farming. It mainly produces Malvasia, a sweet white wine, and capers.**

The caper bushes with their lovely flowers grow all over the place on rocks and walls, but caper vines are also cultivated on the island. The buds and the *cucunci* are mixed with unrefined sea salt which removes the bitter taste and conserves them. In June, you can pick your own ⚑ wild capers!

The coast is mostly pebbly and accessible from land in just a few places (at *Malfa, Pollara* and *Rinella*). In *Pollara*, which consists of just a few cuboid houses, Michael Radford filmed the 1994 multi-award-winning film *Il Postino* (The Postman) staring Philippe Noiret as Pablo Neruda.

EATING & DRINKING

DA ALFREDO

The whole of Salina seems to descend on this harbour bar to enjoy their legendary *granita* – will it be fig, pistachio or watermelon today? Another popular choice is *pane cunzato*, white bread topped with tomatoes, tuna and capers. *Daily in summer | Via Marina Garibaldi | Santa Maria Salina/Loc. Lingua | tel. 090 984 3075 | €*

'NNI LAUSTA

Langoustines and vegetables from their own garden, and it only gets better in the evening with a bar serving good food. *Daily in summer, closed Nov–mid-March | Via Risorgimento 188 | Santa Maria Salina | tel. 090 984 3486 | €–€€€*

SPORT & ACTIVITIES

FOSSA DELLE FELCI

Time to dust off those hiking boots. The obvious trail starts at the harbour *Santa Marina Salina* and zigzags up through the

INSIDER TIP
Dream view included

flowering vegetation of the extinct volcano to 962m, the highest peak in the Aeolian Islands with an extensive panorama. From here, you can go down to Leni and Rinella. Tired legs guaranteed! *J2*

AROUND SALINA

The population of Alicudi and Filicudi, the two distant islands to the west, has fallen dramatically. Sheep and goat farming and wine production are too arduous; as tourist destinations they may well be pretty and great diving grounds, but their distance from the other islands makes day trips that much more difficult.

1 FILICUDI
28km/40 mins by hydrofoil
The island is dry and covered in high grass and reed. A long scree beach starts at the harbour *Filicudi Porto* and extends as far as the cliffs at Capo Graziano, where the walls of a prehistoric settlement of circular huts can be found on the knoll. A road leads across the plateau past fields and clusters of houses to the main settlement on the island, *Pecorini*, and down to the harbour and beach at *Pecorini Mare*. Tip: Most of the coastline with its grottoes, cliffs and rocky pinnacles can only be accessed by boat.

The *Diving Center Delfini (mobile tel. 340 148 4645 | ildelfinifilicudi. com)* in Pecorini is run by Nino Terrano.

Its highlight is the ancient, shell-encrusted amphorae in the *Museo sottomarino*. The restaurant *Villa La Rosa (daily | Via Rosa 24 | Rocca Ciauli | Filicudi Porto | tel. 090 988 9965 | villalarosa.it | €€)* is part of a B&B; the food conjured up by Signora Adelaide is among the best on the island. Gourmets swear by her swordfish carpaccio with caper cream. *J2*

2 ALICUDI
41km/70 mins by hydrofoil
The island is an oasis for anyone looking for utter peace and quiet. There are only 100 people living on Alicudi, with a few mules to transport goods up the steep stairways. The houses – most of which have been abandoned – were built in terraced fields along the main route that leads from the harbour up to the volcanic peak, at a height of 675m. Accommodation and fresh fish is available in private houses or in the one hotel and restaurant on the island. *Hotel Ericusa (May–Sept | tel. 090 988 9902 | alicudihotel.it | €€)* is just a few yards from the harbour. *H2*

STROMBOLI

(K–L1) **Set apart and to the north of the others is the island of ★ Stromboli (pop. 500). Made famous in Roberto Rossellini's scandalous film of the same name, the vibrant town is hard to resist. Many**

mountaineering enthusiasts come here to tackle the fire-breathing volcano, over whose summit a thin plume of smoke always hovers.

The few cuboid houses in *Ginostra* in the south can only be reached by boat and form Italy's most isolated settlement. Buildings straggle the only road towards the north which hosts the island's three villages – *San Vincenzo, Ficogrande* and *Piscità*.

A paved path through the high reeds, which later turns into an unmade path with a few dangerous spots, starts at the lighthouse and leads up to the summit.

Groups of hikers normally set off in the afternoon to reach the top before sunset to enjoy the nocturnal spectacle of sheaves of embers that are catapulted out of the crater at short intervals. Hikers must be accompanied by a mountain guide and

helmets are compulsory. Take torches and a set of new batteries with you and wear warm, windproof clothing! *Virtual walks* on the internet: *swiss educ.ch/stromboli*

You can also reach Stromboli from Naples and in the summer from Tropea in Calabria.

EATING & DRINKING

🔳 LA LAMPARA 🍴
Open-air pizzeria with a pizza chef from Naples. *Daily | Via Vittorio Emanuele | Ficogrande | mobile tel 339 738 9849 | lalamparastromboli.com | €*

🔳 PUNTA LENA 🚩
Exquisite, light, regional cuisine; terrace with pergola and marvellous views. *April–Oct daily | Via Marina 8 | tel. 090 986 204 | ristorantepuntalena stromboli.it | €€€*

Eerily beautiful nocturnal spectacle: lava pours over the flank of Stromboli

AROUND STROMBOLI

5 PANAREA

22km / 25 mins by hydrofoil

Linen dresses and designer sunglasses at the ready! Panarea is a summer hideout for the rich ad famous. It is the smallest and most fashionable of the islands.

The island is surrounded by numerous rocky outcrops and islets that rise from the sea – the remains of a collapsed volcano. The three villages *Ditella*, *San Pietro* with its harbour, and *Drauto* merge into one another, scattered picturesquely up the jet-black rocky slopes. The west coast is inaccessible, whereas a path down the east coast links the hot steaming fumaroles in the north with ★ *Punta Milazzese* in the south. Here, on a ledge 20m above the sea, you can see the walls of a prehistoric village of circular huts. A path leads to the dreamlike bay 🌴 *Cala Junco* surrounded by cliffs. The little island offshore and the rocky cove are the perfect place for swimming, snorkelling and diving.

INSIDER TIP
Try the orange crab

Its unusual take on traditional dishes has brought cult status to the trattoria *Da Pina* (daily | Via San Pietro 3 | tel. 090 983 032 | ristorantedapina.com | €€€), run by cookbook author Pina Mandarano and her family – complete with veranda and garden. In the evening, the jet set enjoys anthroposophical

Picture-perfect holiday: the island of Panarea is small and beautiful

SPORT & ACTIVITIES

Magmatrek is a cooperative of volcano guides – also English-speaking *(Via Vittorio Emanuele | tel. 090 986 5768 | magmatrek.it).* Equipment is available to buy or hire in the sports shop *Totem (Piazza San Vincenzo 4 | tel. 090 986 5752).*

BEACHES

A long scree and gravel beach with black sand in places stretches the length of the three villages on the north coast.

Demeter menus under petroleum lights on the terrace of *Hotel Raya* (May–Oct | tel. 090 983 013 | hotel-raya.it | €€€), with its boutique and open-air club.

If that sounds a little over budget, treat yourself to a one-of-a-kind drink at the harbourside bar *Da Carola (daily | tel. 090 983 161 | €)*: a granita made from peaches, with old Malvasia wine *(pesca e Malvasia)*. Absolutely dreamy! ⬚ K1

INSIDER TIP
Cocktails, but ice cold

VULCANO

(⬚ K2) **The island is pretty rugged and most people come here with the express purpose of summiting a volcano. The holiday island of ★ Vulcano (pop. 450) also owes its popularity to its two sandy bays *Porto Levante* and *Porto Ponente*, where hot fumaroles heat the water in a few select spots.**

Since 2019, however, the rather spartan thermal operation of the infernally sulphurous fumarole pools directly behind the harbour has sadly been discontinued.

A waymarked path (approx. 80 minutes for the ascent) leads up to the main crater, the *Gran Cratere*. Officially closed, the whole world seems to ignore this inconvenient fact at their own peril. The smell of pungent sulphur may well indicate that the volcano is dormant but it is still very much alive deep inside and could well erupt again at any time.

A road along an elevated plain with panoramic views leads to the centre of the island, to *Piano*. A tiny road with hairpin bends carries on to *Gelso lighthouse* right in the south. In summer, boats leave from the pier to nearby *Spiaggia del Asino*. Take your time to enjoy the magnificent view of the north coast of Sicily and the wall-like Nebrodi mountains behind it, with the snow-capped summit of Mount Etna towering above them.

EATING & DRINKING

LA FORGIA DA MAURIZIO
Sicily meets Goa: imaginative seafood dishes near the harbour. *Daily | Strada Provinciale 179 | mobile tel. 33 47 66 00 69 | €–€€*

MARIA TINDARA
Up on the mountain in Piano, sits this traditional restaurant serving rabbit and homemade pasta. *Daily | Via Provinciale 37 | tel. 090 985 3004 | marialindaravulcano.it | € €€*

WHERE TO SLEEP ON LIPARI

DELICIOUSLY RURAL
Simplicity done with love. Family friendly B&B with barbecue area and vegetable patch. At the very private *Villa Angelina (2 rooms | Via S. Croce | Pianoconte | Lipari | tel. 090 982 2244 | €)* you'll be staying with one of the island's most passionate cooks, who is more than happy to share their recipes!

DISCOVERY TOURS

Do you want to get under the skin of the island? Then these discovery tours provide the perfect guide. They include advice on which sights to visit, tips on where to stop for that perfect holiday snap, a choice of the best places to eat and drink and suggestions for fun activities.

❶ VIA DEL SALE

➤ Birdwatch in the lagoon
➤ Discover how sea salt is extracted
➤ Explore a Carthaginian island and tuck into couscous

📍 Trapani	🏁 Marsala
→ 43km	8 hrs (3½ hrs' total riding time)

ℹ Cost: approx. 60 euros per person plus about 50 euros for the taxi.
Important tip: it gets extremely hot in summer; the salt lakes reflect sunlight so don't forget your sunglasses.
To return to Trapani, pre-book a large taxi with Salvatore *(approx. 50 euros | mobile tel. 388 868 0690)*.

Take a look: the windmills of the Ettore Infersa saltworks are open to visitors

WHITE SALT AND PINK FLAMINGOS

In ❶ Trapani ➤ p. 94 *take the SP 21 minor road to Marsala (signposted Airport/Birgi, later Via del Sale). About 5km south of Trapani there is a turning to the* ❷ Salina di Nubia. Here the Culcasi family shows the different stages of traditional salt production and explains the laborious process of pumping up the salt water with Archimedes' screws in the Museo del Sale *(daily 9.30am–7pm | admission incl. tour 7 euros | museodelsale.it | ⊙ 30 mins).* Take in the views of the nearest Aegadian Islands ➤ p. 98 – Favignana and Levanzo – and of the promontory in the north dominated by Erice ➤ p. 95.

Returning to the Strada Provinciale 21, follow the directions for Marsala until you reach the turning to Birgi Novo, *a village beyond the airport of single-storey houses surrounded by vineyards.* Ride along a narrow lane heading south along the banks of the lagoon (stagnone). *Between 30cm and 4m deep, the lagoon has a wealth of underwater flora and is a natural habitat for water birds. In winter, migratory birds like to rest here before flying on to Africa, while in spring flocks of birds from the Maghreb migrate to the milder climate of the*

❶ Trapani

8.5km 35 mins

❷ Salina di Nubia

20km 1 hr 25 mins

5 km
3.10 mi

stagnone. With a bit of luck, you should spot pink flamingos, white herons and the black-winged stilt, which bears the beautiful name of *Cavaliere d'Italia*.

INSIDER TIP
Stopover for migratory birds

GETTING SALTY

On a level with the island of Mozia is the largest operating salt works, ❸ Ettore Infersa *(June–Sept 9am–8pm; April/May, Oct/Nov 9am–5pm; Dec–March 9.30am–3.30pm | tel. 092 373 3003 | seisaline.it)*. You can book various activities, such as a tour of the salt lakes, tastings or a visit to a museum and a windmill. Buy some of the white gold in pretty packaging as a unique souvenir. A few steps further along the quay is ❹ Trattoria Mamma Caura *(daily | tel. 09 23 96 60 36 | seisaline.it | €–€€)* with great views from the terrace. Here you can try the regional speciality *cuscus con pesce*, in fish stock served with a dry white Grillo or Cataratto wine from classic Marsala vines. Lock up your bike and *catch a small ferry over to Mozia (takes approx. 5 mins | April–Oct 9.15am–6.30pm; Nov–March 9.15am–3pm | 5 euros | mozialine.com)*.

❸ **Ettore Infersa**
300m 2 mins

❹ **Trattoria Mamma Caura**

1.5 km 20 mins

❺ **Mozia**

THE CARTHAGINIAN ISLAND

The settlement of ❺ ★ Mozia (Mothya) on the partly wooded island of San Pantaleo was a fortified Phoenician port and important trading hub until its destruction by the Greeks in 397 BCE. Archaeological ruins still exist today. A walk around the island with its profusion of pines, palms and vineyards takes approximately one hour. In the south are the basins and walls of the 2,500-year-old harbour; in the north is the urn graveyard (tophet) with roughly hewn gravestones. At the Cappiddazzu excavation site there once stood a monumental temple to Tanit, the principal deity of the Carthaginians alongside her consort Baal, who turned the island into a strategic base. The villa, once belonging to the English wine magnate and Marsala baron Joseph Whitaker, now houses the museum *(island visit incl. museum and archaeological zones daily 9am–3pm, April–Oct 9.30am–6.30pm | admission 9 euros | fonda zionewhitaker.it)*, with finds from the Punic past of Mozia and Marsala. The highlight is a life-sized marble figure, the *Ephebe of Mozia*, probably a Greek-Punic sculpture from the fifth century BCE of a young male figure dressed in a transparent robe with a wealth of folds.

Returning to the mainland, *follow the coastal road –* passing fishing villages, holiday homes and African-style palm-lined alleys leading to vineyard villas – *back to* ⑥ Marsala ➤ p. 99. Unfortunately, the trains from Marsala don't usually accept bicycles, so instead pre-book a taxi with enough space for bikes and be back in ① *Trapani* in around 40 minutes.

13km 1hr 10 mins

⑥ **Marsala**

Wine tasting with all the trimmings is a must in Marsala

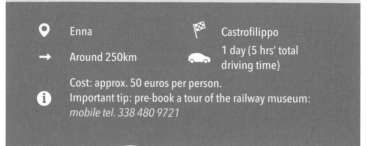

❷ WHEAT FIELDS & SULPHUR MINES

➤ Marvel at nostalgic railways
➤ Chat with locals
➤ Explore mountain villages and cappuccino bars

📍 Enna   🏁 Castrofilippo

→ Around 250km   🚗 1 day (5 hrs' total driving time)

ℹ️ Cost: approx. 50 euros per person.
Important tip: pre-book a tour of the railway museum:
mobile tel. 338 480 9721

❶ Enna

15km 20 mins

❷ Villarosa

STEAM ENGINE HORNS

Route 121 leads from ❶ Enna ➤ p. 65 into the wide valley of the River Salso. The road twists through the countryside here, sometimes on flyovers that are up to 10km long. In ❷ Villarosa there are seven, bright-red freight wagons at the station, which the former station master Primo David has turned into a museum *(Tue–Sun 9.30am–12.30pm and 4.30–7.30pm, by appointment | admission 5 euros | trenomuseovillarosa. com | ⏱ 1 hr)* on the history of the area with relation to the railway, sulphur mining, agriculture and emigration. To date, there are 2,500 objects ranging from a whistle to a prince's bedroom, collected from Villarosa, the rest of Sicily and from all over the world.

MARKET IN THE SULPHUR METROPOLIS

36km 40 mins

❸ Caltanissetta

Take the A 19 motorway south to the former sulphur-mining centre ❸ Caltanissetta. The market stands and narrow alleyways in the old town remind you of an oriental bazaar. Mingle with the "old men's crowd" in the piazza, with the fountain of Neptune in front of the cathedral. Have a bite to eat here before visiting the gigantic, unfinished Baroque Palazzo Moncada, an architectural treasure.

MEDIEVAL FORT & GROTTO SAINTS

Mussomeli is reached *along the narrow, winding road via San Cataldo*. Some 2km before you get there you will pass ❹ Castello Manfredonico which dates from the 12th century and is located on a rocky promontory that made it unassailable. On a clear day you can see most of Sicily from the top. *Continue via Santo Giovanni Gemini and Cammarata* until you reach the Monti Sicani, with their forests and many springs. It is worth making a short detour to the Greek-style pilgrimage church of ❺ Santa Rosalia di Quisquina *(side road on the right 3km before reaching Santo Stefano Quisquina)* where the patron saint of Palermo lived in a cave as a hermit in the 12th century. She was later invoked as a miracle-worker against the plague.

ALBANIAN VILLAGE AND PISTACHIO CAPPUCCINO

From Santo Stefano di Quisquina, drive through Alessandria della Rocca to ❻ San Angelo Muxaro, an Albanian settlement boldly sited on a mountain plateau. Below the town is a waymarked footpath from the road to rock tombs from the pre-Hellenic period. *Continue south* to refreshingly untouristy ❼ Aragona.

52km 1 hr 15 mins	
❹ Castello Manfredonico	
37km 35 mins	
❺ Santa Rosalia di Quisquina	
44km 45 mins	
❻ San Angelo Muxaro	
16km 20 mins	
❼ Aragona	

Take a break at the favourite bar of locals, Pasticceria La Preferita *(Via Roma 217)*, to taste their marzipan *dolci* and cappuccino, which are out of this world and sprinkled with flaked pistachios harvested in the nearby Platani valley! Authentic Sicilian folk art is on display at the Chiesa Madre with its nativity scene filled with lots of crib figures.

INSIDER TIP
Cappuccino speciale!

BAROQUE FINALE

14km 20 mins
8 Favara
15km 15 mins
9 Naro

10 Castrofilippo
15km 15 mins

The route now transports you through a landscape of artistic interpretations, taking you to the Baroque rural towns of 8 Favara *and* 9 Naro. *Here, sculptors and stonemasons let their fantasies run wild, carving faces, masks, grotesque caryatids, pillars, sills and squiggles out of the soft, dark-yellow sandstone to adorn the façades of churches and palaces. Finish your tour with an evening* cena *of stuffed cabbage and quail at* Osteria Cacciatore *(closed Wed and lunchtime except on Sun | Via Puglia 5 | tel. 092 282 9824 | €) in nearby* 10 Castrofilippo, *which is run by five sisters.*

Snow-covered Etna makes a stark contrast to the gently rolling hills around Enna

❸ THE GREEN GIANTS

➤ Picnic in a shepherd's hut
➤ Walk under holly trees
➤ See half of Sicily from above

📍	Piano Sempria	🏁	Piano Sempria
🔄	3.5km	🥾	3 hrs (1½ hrs' total hiking time)
📊	Easy	↗	180m

ℹ Cost: 25 euros per person
Important tips: you can buy everything you need for a picnic in Castelbuono. Information also available at *parcodellemadonie.it*

PANORAMIC ENTRANCE

The start of this mountain hike is ❶ Piano Sempria (1,260m), which you can reach from Castelbuono ➤ p. 89 along a *10km-long mountain road*. An information board at the beginning of the path *(sentiero natura)* shows the route. At the hollow, 800-year-old oak, in which there is a small statue of the Virgin Mary, the *path crosses the road and zig-zags its way up through the steep oak woodland to a* viewpoint.

❶ Piano Sempria

1km 1 hr

PICNIC ON THE PLATEAU

The climb finishes here and *the path continues below a rock face along the slope and runs into a track which passes over a gate onto the grassy* ❷ Piano Pomo (1,380m). There is a *pagghiaru (pagliaio)* here – an elongated stone building with a roof of brushwood, with tables and benches inside. It was built for forest workers and hikers along the lines of a Sicilian shepherd's hut and is the perfect place for a relaxed morning picnic.

❷ Piano Pomo

IN THE HOLLY FOREST

Climb over the fence using the wooden steps and after a few metres down a path you'll come to a grove of giant

700m 30 mins.

holly trees *(Aquifoli giganti)*. These trees have their origins in the Ice Age. Around 100 of the trees are estimated to be 300 years old and more. It is quite dark among the thick trunks as little light penetrates the dense foliage which prompts local hiking guides to call it the *"cattedrale della natura"*. Beyond the grove next to an ancient beech tree *(faggio secolare), an easily recognisable path on the right leads through beech and oak woodland,* with equally huge tree trunks, to the cross on the summit of ❸ Cozzo Luminario (1,512m), from which you have an all-round panoramic view, taking in the sea, the

INSIDER TIP
An unusual view of Etna

Aeolian Islands, Etna and the high plateau of Pizzo Carbonara (1,979m).

❸ Cozzo Luminario	
300m	5 mins.
❹ Piano Imperiale	
1,5km	25 mins.
❶ Piano Sempria	

PASTA IN A MOUNTAIN HUT

The path then descends into a dip in the karst rocks of ❹ Piano Imperiale, and from there *onto the forest track that will bring you back to* ❶ Piano Sempria. Hearty food, such as tagliatelle with mushrooms and pork from free-range pigs, is on offer at the mountain lodge Rifugio Francesco Crispi *(28 beds | tel. 092 167 2279 | €)* run by the Club Alpino Siciliano..

❹ VIEWS OF CALABRIA & THE COAST

➤ See Sicily's greatest paintings
➤ Eat mussels by the lagoon
➤ Experience a bird's eye view of the Strait of Messina

📍	Messina	🏁	Messina
🔄	Around 75km	🚗	8½ hours (1½ hrs' total driving time)
ℹ️	Cost: 45 euros per person What to pack: swimwear, binoculars		

DOWN TO THE MUSEUM

Start at the cathedral square in ❶ Messina ➤ p. 53 and *follow the coastal road Viale della Libertà north to no. 465* (parking spaces available on the opposite side of the road). Enjoy an almost private viewing of two of Caravaggio's master paintings in the picture gallery of the Museo Regionale Mume ➤ p. 54, *Adoration of the Shepherds* and *The Raising of Lazarus*, both painted in 1609 and impressive for their chiaroscuro technique, their realism and their poignancy.

 ❶ Messina

OFF TO THE MUSSEL LAGOON

Back on the Viale della Libertà, take a left shortly after the museum uphill along the Via della Annunziata and then follow the panoramic SP 43 north until you reach the fishing village of ❷ Ganzirri. What was once a spot for wallowing wild boar is now two lagoons *(pantano grande/piccolo)* that are famous for mussel *(cozze)* farming. Locals swear by the eel patties, swordfish *involtini* and *spaghetti con vongole* served at the Trattoria del Lago *(closed Fri and in the evenings | Via Lago Grande 92 | tel. 090 392 275 | trattoriadellago.it | €€)* which has been serving *cucina messine* for more than 50 years.

11km 15 mins

❷ Ganzirri

Lipari, Vulcano
Rinella, Salina   Panarea

Capo Rasocolmo   ACQUARONE
SPARTA   ⑤   ④
SANTA SABA
113 dir.   Casa Bianca   Punta del Faro
SINDARO MARINA   Massa   o Capo Peloro   Stromboli
San Giorgio   Massa San Nicolò   MORTELLE
Massa   FARO   4.5 101 COLONIE   ③
Monte Pace   Santa Lucia   SUPERIORE   Pantano   TORRE FAR
419   Massa   320   ②   Grande
CASTANEA   Massa San Giovanni   CURCURACI   415   GANZIRRI
DELLEFURIE   422   SANT'AGATA
Orto Liuzzo   SALICE   Trivio   GROTTA   Cannitello
Monte Ciccia   Rizzotti   PACE
609   CONTEMPLAZIONE   Villa
GESSO   Urni   SANTISSIMA   PARADISO   Salerno, Napoli, Genova, Civitavecchia
ause   ANNUNZIATA   SALVATORE   San Giovanni   Piale
Serro   San   DEI GRECI   (15)
Settentrionale   Nicolò   ⑧   Acciarello   Camp
Calvaruso   Sicula   ⑥   BADIAZZA   Calabro
113   E90   MESSINA
⑨   Fiera   (3)
CATARRATTI   Sant.   Concessa
Pizzo Chiarino   CAMARO   Montalto   CATONA   A2
841   CASALOTTO   Duomo
Nunziatella   BORDONARO
CUMIA   SANTO
San Filippo   GALLICO MARINA
Superiore   GAZZI
Dinnammare   San Filippo   CONTESSE   Archi
⑦   Inferiore   E45   SANTA
1127   Zafferia   LUCIA
LARDERIA   PISTUNINA
Tripoldo   A18   TREMESTIERI

2 km
1.24 mi

SEE ANCIENT SEA MONSTERS

After your mussel feast, *head to the coast along the increasingly narrowing strait to Sicily's most northeasterly point,* ③ Punta del Faro, or Capo Peloro as it was called in Antiquity. From the beach of the Horcynus Orca cultural centre *(horcynusorca.it)* you can see the Rock of Scilla on the other side of the strait and the whirlpools just off the coast that form in the shallows and along the sandbanks of Cariddi. They pose a danger to small ships even today. In Homeric mythology they ate sailors as the sea monsters Scylla and Charybdis. This is where the 3km bridge across the

5km 7 mins

③ Punta del Faro

shallow banks was to be built before the project was cancelled in 2013, soon after it had been started.

GAZE AT THE CALABRIAN MAINLAND

From the Punta del Faro, *head west* to visit tiny seaside resorts such as ❹ Acquarone with numerous bathing areas and a craggy coastline interspersed with sandy and pebble beaches heading to ❺ Spartà, Sicily's northernmost point. *The road then runs along the ridge of the Peloritani mountains to* ❻ Colle San Rizzo (624 m) *and along the same road to* ❼ Monte Antennamare, 1,130m above sea level, where there is a pilgrimage church dedicated to the Virgin Mary. The view from up here takes in the Tyrrhenian Sea and the north of Sicily, the Aeolian Islands and, to the east, Messina, the strait and Calabria's southern headland. To the south and west you can make out the mountain valleys and peaks of Monti Peloritani. The woods in the vicinity with cool springs and picnic places are the ideal spot for a relaxing break.

Returning to Colle San Rizzo, it is worth making a detour halfway back to Messina, to ❽ Badiazza, the romantic ruins of a fortified church with a tower and battlements from the Norman period.

SICILY'S MOST ICONIC PANINO

To end the tour, join the queue and try some local fast food at the authentic and highly recommended ❾ Kiosk Don Minico (*donminico.com*) *at the crossroads with the SS 113*. With over 70 years' history, they serve spicy *pane della disgraziata* stuffed full with goat's cheese, salami, capers, dried tomatoes, olives and artichokes from the island of Filicudi: fast food at its finest! Now *return to the port of* ❶ Messina ➤ p. 53 *along the steep winding SS 113.*

INSIDER TIP
Messina's most popular snack

11km 11 mins	
❹ Acquarone	
3km 4 mins	
❺ Spartà	
14km 13min	
❻ Colle San Rizzo	
9km 9 mins	
❼ Monte Antennamare	
11km 11 mins	
❽ Badiazza	
2km 3 mins	
❾ Kiosk Don Minico	
10km 12 mins	
❶ Messina	

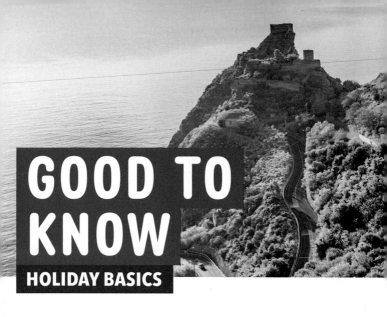

GOOD TO KNOW
HOLIDAY BASICS

ARRIVAL

GETTING THERE

Although it can take forever to drive down through Italy, the journey by motorway is spectacular. After years of construction work, the mountain highway running from Salerno to Reggio di Calabria has finally more or less opened. Alternatives are the car ferries

RESPONSIBLE TRAVEL

Are you aware of your carbon footprint while travelling? You can offset your emissions (*myclimate. org*), plan your route with the environment in mind (*routerank.com*) and go gently on both nature and culture. If you would like to find out more about eco-tourism please refer to *ecotourism.org*.

Genoa–Palermo, Civitavecchia–Termini Imerese and Naples–Palermo. Prices, timetables and reservations are listed under *traghetti.com* and *gnv.it*

Travelling by train from the UK involves several changes – in Italy, either in Milan or Rome. There are no direct lines through Europe. The cost of a sleeper and supplements for intercity trains usually make the journey more expensive than flying. *trenitalia.it* or *seat61.com*

A number of different airlines fly from the UK and Ireland directly to Sicily (usually Palermo or Catania). These include British Airways, Ryanair, easyJet, TUI and Aer Lingus. Direct buses run from the airport in Catania *(aeroporto.catania.it)* to Messina, Taormina, Ragusa, Enna, Cefalù, Agrigento and Syracuse; from Palermo airport *(gesap.it)* to Trapani. There's also an airport in Trapani *(airg-est.it)*. Comiso airport in the southeast

The road to Forza d'Agrò is toll-free – but don't forget the speed limit!

is currently only connected to a few mainland Italian airports and Bucarest (*aeroportodicomiso.eu*).

GETTING IN

Visas are not required for EU citizens; citizens of the UK, US or Canada require a visa only if staying for longer than three months. Passports are required when checking into hotels and campsites.

CLIMATE & WHEN TO GO

On the coast, the Mediterranean climate promises long, hot, dry summers. The best months to travel are May, June, September and October when the temperatures are pleasant, the sea warm and you miss the mass invasion of tourists in the high season and Easter week. The winters are mild and wet; many hotels and restaurants close at this time of year. *tempoitalia.it*

GETTING AROUND

CAR HIRE

Major car rental companies can be found in Palermo, Catania, Syracuse, Messina, Taormina and at the airports. Prices are from around 150–400 euros per week if you book on the internet before you travel to Italy. Booking locally costs around 25% more.

DRIVING

The maximum speed in built-up areas is 50kmh, on main roads 90kmh, on dual carriageways 110kmh, and 130kmh on motorways (110kmh in the rain; 50kmh in fog). Drivers and all passengers must wear seatbelts. It is mandatory to drive with dipped head lights outside built-up areas during the day. There must be an emergency jacket in the car. It is recommended that you take a Green Card insurance document with you. The blood alcohol concentration limit is 0.5mg/alcohol per 100ml/blood (or 0.0mg if your license is less than three years old).

Yes, Italy is a relaxed country, but if you get caught, you'll pay for all those who slip through the net. Speeding offences of more than 40kmh and drunk driving (more than 1.5mg/alcohol per 100ml/blood) will cost you 530 euros, your licence and the car, which is then auctioned off. This also applies to non-Italians and hire cars too!

In many places, no-parking zones are only marked with coloured lines on the edge of the pavement. No markings means unrestricted parking, unless signs tell you something else; yellow means reserved for the police, the *carabinieri* and local buses; black and yellow means no parking; blue means pay-and-display. Tickets can usually be bought in bars, shops and kiosks. You have to scratch the respective fields to show the time and date. In cities, self-appointed parking attendants will guide you to a free space for a moderate tip (sometimes they will keep the key to manoeuvre for you). These helpers are usually trustworthy so you can use their services, but do not leave any valuables in your car.

PUBLIC TRANSPORT
Sicily has an extensive railway network that is mostly single track. Local trains usually only have second-class carriages. Intercity and express trains often run late and many stations are some distance from the village or town centre.

An extensive bus network, operated by a host of private companies, supplements and/or replaces the lack of a good railway system. In many towns, however, there is no central bus station. For more information on bus routes and connections see *anavsicilia.it*

TAXI
In Sicily's larger urban centres taxis have meters. A tip of 5–10% is usual. In small villages and in the countryside you are best advised to agree on a price with the driver before setting off.

ELECTRICITY – ADAPTER TYPES C, F & L

Current is 220 volts. You'll need a Southern Europe adapter with two or three round prongs. In older hotels sometimes only flat plugs fit, in which case hotel reception will usually provide an adapter.

EMERGENCIES

CONSULATES & EMBASSIES
BRITISH EMBASSY
Via XX Settembre 80A | 00187 Rome | tel. +39 064 220 0001 | gov.uk/world/italy
US CONSULATE GENERAL
Piazza della Repubblica | 80122 Napoli | tel. +39 081 583 8111 | it.usembassy. gov/embassy-consulates/naples/

FESTIVALS & EVENTS
ALL YEAR ROUND

FEBRUARY
Sant'Agata (Catania): procession of the patron saint of Etna (3–5 February), *festadisantagata.it*

FEBRUARY/MARCH
Almond Blossom Festival (Agrigento): with music, *mandorloinfiore.online*
Carnival processions (Sciacca and Acireale): *sciaccarnevale.it* and *carnevaleacireale.eu*

EASTER
Processione dei Misteri (Trapani): night-time penitential procession (Good Friday), *unionemaestranze.it*
The Dance of the Devils (Prizzi): garish spectacle to chase out the winter (Easter Sunday)

MAY
Sant'Alfio (Trecastagni): parade of Sicilian carts (around 10 May)
Infiorata (Noto): stairways are decorated in designs made of flower petals (third Sunday in May), *infiorata dinoto.it*

MAY–JULY
Greek Theatre Festival (Syracuse): *indafondazione.org*

MID-JUNE–SEPTEMBER
Taormina Arte: (Taormina): cinema and concerts at the Teatro Greco, *taoarte.it*

14/15 JULY
U Fistinu (Palermo): festival of Santa Rosalia, with fair and concerts

12-14 AUGUST
Palio dei Normanni: (Piazza Armerina): medieval-themed riding tournaments, *paliodeinormanni.com* (photo)

MID/LATE SEPTEMBER
Couscous Festival (San Vito Lo Capo): chefs from both North Africa and the Mediterranean compete, *couscousfest.it*

DECEMBER
Santa Lucia (Syracuse): procession and festival of light (13 December)
Presepi viventi (many mountain towns): live Nativity scenes (Advent)

EMBASSY OF CANADA

Via Zara 30 | 00198 Rome | tel. +39 068 5444 2911 | canada.it

HEALTH

For citizens of the EU, the European insurance card EHIC entitles you to treatment (sometimes with additional fees). Visitors from non-EU countries should take out private insurance. Further information is available at *fit-fortravel.nhs.uk*

EMERGENCY SERVICES

Accident/police: *tel. 112 and 113*
Ambulance: *tel. 118*
Breakdown assistance: *mobile tel. 800 116 800 or tel. 039 21041*
Fire brigade and forest fires: *tel. 115 and 1515*
Coast guard: *tel. 1530*

ESSENTIALS

ACCOMMODATION

The star categories (one for simple, five for luxury) only give a vague idea of facilities and prices. Two-star options are often far more charming than the overhyped competition. Room rates must be posted. There is a wide range of B&Bs (often in historic buildings) where "breakfast" is a meal voucher for the bar next door. If the owner appears in person, this is your chance to experience the island from a local's perspective.

ADMISSION

Most state museums and historic/ excavation sites cost between 4 and 19 euros; EU citizens under 18 have free admission; young people aged between 18 and 25 are entitled to a 25–50% discount (first Sunday of the month free). Entrance is free to many small museums, but donations are welcome. Custodians who unlock churches and palaces should be given a tip of around 5–10 euros.

AGRITURISMO 🐒

Holidaying on a farm has become a popular, low-cost and child-friendly concept throughout Italy; it gives visitors a chance to get to know an area and the people better. On Sicily, with its feudal structure, *agriturismo* often means staying in historic country houses. Many farms have mountain bikes and/or horses and can organise excursions. Virtually all *agriturismi* serve good country food – after all, they have to produce their own food to be certified. Information under *agriturismo-sicilia.it*

BEACHES & SWIMMING

Carefully laid-out sunbeds, such in the *stabilimenti* on the Adriatic, are more typical of the beaches around Taormina. Otherwise sunbathing on Sicily is a pretty relaxed affair and up to each individual. The rental price of sunshades *(ombrello)* and sunbeds *(lettino, sdraio)* is reasonable by Italian standards. In resorts mainly frequented by Italians, the season can be relatively short (June–mid-September). Even though many Sicilian women prefer to go topless and nude bathing is accepted on many beaches such as Torre Salsa near Siculiana, the only official nudist beach (since 2016) is Bulala at Gela.

CAMPING

There are around 100 campsites on Sicily and the nearby islands. Most are on the coast and are open between Easter and the end of October *(camp-ing.it)*. In addition, there are hundreds of places for staying overnight in your motorhome, e.g. carparks at beaches that are often free but have no facilities. There are also a few fee-paying sites for motorhomes with washing facilities, roofs for shade and trees. Info: *womo66.com*

COOKING LESSONS

Sicilian cooking is booming and there are a variety of 🌂 cooking courses available. The *padrona* of *Agriturismo San Leonardello (Via Madonna della Libertà 165 | tel. 095 964 020 | san leonardello.it)* in Giarre reveals how to get the hole in the *maccheroni*. Those interested in learning the secrets behind the world-renowned *pasticce-ria siciliana* can take part in the cannoli cooking class organised by *Pasticceria d'Amore (see p. 52)* in Taormina.

CRIME

The Mafia has better things to do than rob tourists. In fact, it's rumoured they make a pretty penny from the travel business. Petty theft from moped *(scippo)* drivers in Palermo has plum-meted, meaning Sicily can be considered a very safe travel region,

and not just inland. That said, never leave valuables on display in your car either in big cities or on the beach and it is best to use car parks with surveillance.

CUSTOMS

There are no longer any allowance restrictions for EU citizens on tax-free items. If you are arriving from a non-EU country, different regulations apply. Check the internet before leaving home. For tax and duty on goods brought to the UK see: *gov.uk/uk-border-control*

OPENING HOURS

Shops, supermarkets and department stores are generally open from 8.30am–1pm and 4/5–8pm. Shops close one afternoon a week – this varies from shop to shop. During the high season, most shops in tourist areas are open all day and some well into the night. Trattorias usually open 1–3pm and 8–10.30pm. Clubs usually open after 10pm. Garages are often closed on Sundays and after 8pm, and some-times at lunchtime.

POST

Stamps *(francobolli)* are available from post offices and sometimes from tobacconists *(tabacchi)*. Letters and postcards by *posta prioritaria* within Italy cost 95 cents and 1 euro for else-where within Europe.

PRICES

Sicily is a middling-priced tourist des-tination compared to other areas in Italy. An espresso drunk standing in a bar costs less than 1 euro virtually everywhere, a glass of mineral water 50 cents, a beer or an aperitif 3–6 euros. In popular tourist centres, being seated and served at a table can cost two or three times as much. You must budget for between 25 and 50 euros for a full meal (fish is rather expensive) – but even if you splash out the bill will seldom come to more than 60 euros.

Watch out: filling up with petrol can cost up to 30 cents/litre more if you go to a larger petrol station and don't use a *servizio-self-service* pump. Small petrol stations offer this service free of charge.

ATMs *(bancomat, postamat)* can be found throughout Sicily, including in some small villages off the beaten track. Not all hotels, restaurants, garages and shops take credit cards. MasterCard and Visa are widely accepted on Sicily.

PUBLIC HOLIDAYS

1 Jan	New Year's Day
6 Jan	Epiphany
1 April 2024, 21 April 2025	Easter Monday *(Pasquetta)*
25 April	Anniversary of the Liberation from Fascism
1 May	Labour Day
2 June	Founding of the Republic
15 Aug	Assumption Day
1 Nov	All Saints' Day
8 Dec	Immaculate Conception
25 Dec	Christmas
26 Dec	*Santo Stefano*

HOW MUCH DOES IT COST

Tomatoes	*1–10 euros for 1 kg in summer, depending on the variety*
Coffee	*from 80 cents for an espresso at the bar*
Wine	*5–8 euros for a carafe (¼ litre)*
Petrol	*2–2.10 euros for 1 litre of super*
Coppola	*approx. 50 euros for a designer cap*
Town buses	*1.40–1.80 euros per trip*

TELEPHONE

The mobile phone is called *cellulare* or *telefonino* in Italian. If you intend phoning a lot within Italy, it's worth buying an Italian SIM card. These can be bought in any phone shop, even if you have no Italian tax number *(codice fiscale)*. A photocopy of your passport is needed.

The country code for Italy is 0039. It is necessary to dial the 0 at the beginning of each fixed-line connection – both from abroad and when making local calls.

TOILETS

Public toilets are few and far between and not usually in pristine condition. It is quite normal to drink a quick espresso before using the *bagno* in a bar – in an emergency you can simply place a *mancia* of 50 cents on the bar.

Signore is the plural of *signora*; a *signore* should head for the gents marked *Signori*!

TOURIST INFORMATION
IN THE UK
Italian National Tourist Board: 1 Princes Street, London W1B 2AY | italia. it/en
For general information on Sicily, see: *visitsicily.info*

ON SICILY
The offices run by the *Servizio Turistico Regionale (STR)* can be found in the provincial capitals and in major holiday centres. Smaller towns often have seasonal pro-loco offices: *regione. sicilia.it*.

CARABINIERI
COMANDO STAZIONE
SQUADRA P.G.

ORARIO
Apertura Al Pubblico
Dalle Ore 8.30 Alle Ore 17.00
Dalle Ore 08.00 Alle Ore 14.00
In Mancanza Di Risposta
Telefonare
Al 112

WEATHER IN CATANIA

■ High season
■ Low season

	JAN	FEB	MARCH	APRIL	MAY	JUNE	JULY	AUG	SEPT	OCT	NOV	DEC
Daytime temperature	14°	15°	17°	19°	23°	28°	31°	31°	28°	23°	19°	16°
Night-time temperature	8°	8°	9°	12°	15°	19°	22°	23°	20°	16°	13°	9°
☀	4	5	6	7	8	10	11	10	8	7	6	4
🌂	9	5	6	4	3	2	1	1	3	7	7	8
≋	15°	14°	14°	15°	17°	21°	24°	25°	24°	22°	19°	16°

☀ Hours of sunshine per day   🌂 Rainy days per month   ≋ Water temperature in °C

WORDS & PHRASES IN ITALIAN

SMALL TALK

We have indicated the stressed vowel by a dot under the vowel.

yes/no/maybe	sì/no/forse
please/thank you	per favore/grazie
Excuse me/sorry!	Scusa!/Scusi!
Pardon?	Come dice?/Prego?
Good morning/good day/good evening/good night!	Buon giorno!/Buon giorno!/Buona sera!/Buona notte!
Hello/Bye/Goodbye!	Ciao!/Ciao!/Arrivederci!
My name is …	Mi chiamo …
What is your name? (formal/informal)	Come si chiama?/Come ti chiami?
I would like … /Do you have …?	Vorrei …/Avete …?
I (don't) like this	(Non) mi piace.
good/bad	buono/cattivo

SYMBOLS

EATING & DRINKING

The menu, please!	Il menù, per favore.
bottle/jug/glass	bottiglia/caraffa/bicchiere
knife/fork/spoon	coltello/forchetta/cucchiaio
salt/pepper/sugar	sale/pepe/zucchero
vinegar/oil/milk/cream/lemon	aceto/olio/latte/panna/limone
with/without ice/fizz (in water)	con/senza ghiaccio/gas
cold/too salty/undercooked	freddo/troppo salato/non cotto
vegetarian/allergy	vegetariano/vegetariana/allergia
I would like to pay, please	Vorrei pagare, per favore.
bill/receipt/tip	conto/ricevuta/mancia
cash/debit card/credit card	in contanti/carta di credito

MISCELLANEOUS

Where can I find ...?	Dove posso trovare ...?
left/right/straight	sinistra/destra/dritto
What time is it?	Che ora è? Che ore sono?
it's three o'clock/ it's half three	Sono le tre./Sono le tre e mezza.
today/tomorrow/yesterday	oggi/domani/ieri
How much is ...?	Quanto costa ...?
too much/much/little/everything/nothing	troppo/molto/poco/tutto/niente
expensive/cheap/price	caro/economico/prezzo
Where can I get internet/WiFi?	Dove trovo un accesso internet/wi-fi?
open/closed	aperto/chiuso
broken/it's not working	guasto/non funziona
broken down/garage	guasto/officina
schedule/tickets	orario/biglietto
train/tracks/platform	treno/binario/banchina
Help!/Look out!/Be careful!	Aiuto!/Attenzione!/Prudenza!
ban/forbidden/danger/dangerous	divieto/vietato/pericolo/pericoloso
pharmacy/drug store	farmacia
fever/pain	febbre/dolori
0/1/2/3/4/5/6/7/8/9/10/ 100/1000	zero/uno/due/tre/quattro/cinque / sei/sette/otto/nove/dieci/cento/ mille

HOLIDAY VIBES
FOR RELAXATION & CHILLING

FOR BOOKWORMS & FILM BUFFS

📖 INSPECTOR MONTALBANO

… is a book and TV series. The talented chief inspector loves good, honest food and enjoys flirting with women. The cases he tackles are set in provincial Sicily, where the author Andrea Camilleri grew up.

🎥 CINEMA PARADISO

Oscar-winning film shot in writer and director Giuseppe Tornatore's hometown of Bagheria, as well as other locations on the island. It tells the story of an acclaimed movie director from Rome who recalls his childhood in Sicily (1988).

🎥📖 THE LEOPARD

Claudia Cardinale and Alain Delon star in Luchino Visconti's 1963 classic film adaptation of the best-selling novel. *Il Gattopardo*, by Giuseppe Tomasi di Lampedusa, is an aristocratic saga about Sicilian life and society during the *Risorgimento* (unification of Italy).

🎥 IL POSTINO

Filmed in part on the beautiful Aeolian Islands, this classic film tells the story of a postman who is introduced to literature by famous Chilean poet Pablo Neruda (1994).

PLAYLIST

0:58

‖ **ELFO** – SANGUE CATANESE
Generation 1990: youthful dreams, poverty and the Mafia

▶ **MARIA CALLAS** – CASTA DIVA
Vincenzo Bellini's aria from *Norma*

▶ **DOMENICO MODUGNO** – VITTI NA CROZZA
Garibaldian folk classic sung by an old star

▶ **CARMEN CONSOLI** – STRANIZZA D'AMURI
Love in the time of war, interpreted by the singer-songwriter from Catania

▶ **ROSA BALISTRERI** – LA BARUNISSA DI CARINI
"Palermo's Piaf" sings this morality tale of broken hearts

The holiday soundtrack is available at **Spotify** under **MARCO POLO Italy**

Or scan the code with the Spotify app

ONLINE

VISITSICILY.INFO
Official portal of the Office for Tourism, Sport and Theatre, with suggested itineraries and information on the island's attractions as well as history, art and culture (in English). Appealing photos and up-to-date calendar of events.

WINECODE SICILIA
A useful app from the Istituto Regionale del Vino e dell'Olio Regione Siciliana suggesting winery tours and listing Sicily's most interesting wineries (in English).

LAROSAWORKS.COM
Atmospheric pictures and detailed movie, music and reading lists for tailor-made Island tours created by New Yorker Karen La Rosa.

RICETTE SICILIANI COLLANA
Pasta alla norma and *cassata* to make at home: Sicilian recipes including a list of ingredients and degrees of difficulty, in Italian/English/French.

TRAVEL PURSUIT

THE MARCO POLO HOLIDAY QUIZ

Do you know what makes Sicily tick? Here you can test your knowledge of the little secrets and idiosyncrasies of the island and its people. You will find the correct answers below, with further details on pages 18 to 23 of this guide.

❶ Which opera features in the film *The Godfather III*?
a) *The Sicilian Vespers*, by Giuseppe Verdi
b) *The Novice of Palermo* by Richard Wagner
c) *Cavalleria Rustican* by Pietro Mascagni

❷ The island of Lampedusa ...
a) is only 138km from Tunisia
b) is a port of call for refugees arriving by boat
c) is a popular holiday destination

❸ Which isn't the name of a puppet knight?
a) Rinaldo
b) Carmelo
c) Orlando

❹ Trinacria ...
a) is an ancient Sicilian symbol
b) looks like a winged female head with four legs
c) is used by Birra di Messina as an advertising logo

❺ What is *pizzo*?
a) Sicilian for a slice of pizza
b) A dry southerly wind
c) Protection money

The Trinacria: the coat of arms of Sicily

❻ What is *omertà*?
a) A provincial vegetable dish from Caltanissetta
b) A pledge of secrecy
c) A Sicilian term of endearment for women

❼ In Sicilian sign language, a short nod of the head and click of the tongue means:
a) Get lost!
b) Yes
c) No

❽ How many nature reserves are there on Sicily?
a) Over 100
b) Over 70
c) 30

❾ Which musicians are Sicilian?
a) Adriano Celentano
b) Rosa Balistreri
c) Domenico Modugno

❿ Flat caps …
a) are called *coppola* in Sicily
b) used to be a Mafia identifier
c) are hip in Hollywood

⓫ Which volcanoes are visibly active?
a) Vulcano
b) Etna
c) Stromboli

⓬ What does *passeggiata* mean?
a) An evening encounter
b) A promenade by the sea
c) A tomato

145

INDEX

WE WANT TO HEAR FROM YOU!

Did you have a great holiday? Is there something on your mind? Whatever it is, let us know! Whether you want to praise the guide, alert us to errors or give us a personal tip – MARCO POLO would be pleased to hear from you. Please contact us by email:

sales@heartwoodpublishing.co.uk

We do everything we can to provide the very latest information for your trip. Nevertheless, despite all of our authors' thorough research, errors can creep in. MARCO POLO does not accept any liability for this.

PICTURE CREDITS

Cover photo: Lipari, View from Belvedere Quattrocchi (huber-images: J. Huber)
Photos: DuMont Bildarchiv: Feldhoff/Martin (46, 68, 88, 97, 135), S. Lubenow (11, 20, 27, 50/51, 112, 123); F.M. Frei (8), R. Freyer (45, 67); huber-images: A. Bartuccio (2/3, 9, 28, 56/57, 62, 74/75, 85, 87, 90/91), M. Bortoli (back cover flap, 35, 108/109), C. Cassaro (95), G. Filippini (114, 118), Gräfenhain (54, 71), Liese (105), S. Lubenow (72), M. Ripani (101), A. Saffo (outer front cover flap, inner front cover flap/1, 6/7, 14/15, 38/39, 48, 53, 106, 132/133, 142/143), V. Sciosia (12/13), G. Simeone (10), L. Vaccarella (30/31); La Terra Magica: Lenz (117); Laif: D. Schwelle (82), I. Sciaccia (24/25); Laif/Contrasto: G. Gerbasi (19); Laif/Le Figaro Magazine: S. Frances (98), Martin (103); Laif/robertharding: M. Simoni (32/33); mauritius images/Alamy (126), S. Koval (26/27), R. Lo Savio (81), L. Scamporlino/RealyEasyStar (31); mauritius images/CuboImages (44); mauritius images/imagebroker: Bahnmüller (144/145); P. Peter (147); picture-alliance: D. Parra Saiani (23); picture-alliance/imagebroker: M. Jung (120/121); Shutterstock/Barbara Wheeler (139)

4th Edition – fully revised and updated 2023
Worldwide Distribution: Heartwood Publishing Ltd, Bath, United Kingdom
www.heartwoodpublishing.co.uk

Authors: Hans Bausenhardt, Peter Peter
Editor: Franziska Kahl
Picture editor: Anja Schlatterer
Cartography: © MAIRDUMONT, Ostfildern (pp. 36-37, 122, 125, 128, 130, inner flap, outer flap, pull-out map); ©MAIRDUMONT, Ostfildern, using data from OpenStreetMap, Licence CC-BY-SA 2.0 (pp. 40-41, 42, 58-59, 60, 76-77, 78-79, 92-93, 94, 110-111).
Cover design and pull-out map cover design: bilekjaeger_Kreativagentur with Zukunftswerkstatt, Stuttgart
Page design: Lucia Rojas

Heartwood Publishing credits:
Translated from the German by Madeleine Taylor-Laidler, Susan Jones, Christopher Wynne
Editors: Felicity Laughton, Kate Michell, Sophie Blacksell Jones
Prepress: Summerlane Books, Bath
Printed In India

MARCO POLO AUTHOR
PETER PETER

If he hadn't fallen for the rush of colours and aromas of the Sicilian markets, Peter Peter would probably never have become a university lecturer on the culture of food. He plans and accompanies culinary trips to Italy, raves about Catania's *gelato* in his *Cultural History of Italian Cuisine* and sometimes finds himself swearing in Sicilian as he updates this volume.
pietropietro.de

DOS & DON'TS

HOW TO AVOID SLIP-UPS & BLUNDERS

DON'T PLAY WITH FIRE
Year after year, fires destroy woods and olive groves and threaten houses and even whole villages. Cigarette butts, picnic fires, the hot exhaust of your car parked on dry grass or leaves can all have catastrophic consequences.

DO BE GENEROUS
In virtually no other region in Europe do people tip as generously as in Sicily – the average is 10 per cent. Locals are only too aware of the precarious situation of waiting staff who are not always paid the basic wage. The same applies at the bar: place a coin on your receipt *(scontrino)* and you will be rewarded with a smile and good service.

DON'T SPLIT THE BILL
The *cameriere* won't take kindly to this. First, because it's more work. Second, it's seen as wrong to eat together and then pay separately. If you don't want to be seen as uncivilised, come to an agreement with your tablemates. The ideal solution is to *pagare alla romana*, where everyone puts roughly what they owe down on the table. It almost always works!

DON'T DRIVE INTO THE CENTRE
For some, it is the ultimate kick; for others, a nerve-racking experience. Driving in the cities of Palermo and Catania with the constant beeping of horns, hair-raising overtaking, potholes and not a parking space in sight is not for the faint-hearted.

DO DRESS MODESTLY
Sicily appears to be a laid-back place, but the basic rules of etiquette and decency still apply. Although increasingly more people go topless on beaches, you should cover up a little more in towns and even at the beach trattoria.